Painful Birth

How Chile Became a Free and Prosperous Society

James Rolph Edwards

University Press of America,® Inc.
Lanham • Boulder • New York • Toronto • Plymouth, UK

Copyright © 2013 by University Press of America,® Inc.
4501 Forbes Boulevard, Suite 200, Lanham, Maryland 20706
UPA Aquisitions Department (301) 459-3366

10 Thornbury Road, Plymouth PL6 7PP, United Kingdom

British Library Cataloguing in Publication Information Available

Library of Congress Control Number: 2012947673
ISBN: 978-0-7618-5999-4 (cloth : paper)—ISBN: 978-0-7618-6000-6 (electronic)
ISBN: 978-0-7618-6509-4 (pbk : paper)

Contents

Preface

The Nature of Freedom and a Free Society

Since this book is about how, in the early 1970s, the nation of Chile narrowly escaped becoming a communist tyranny and then was transformed over time into the free and prosperous nation that it is today, it may help to begin by clarifying just what the author means by those terms. Freedom is one of those conditions like democracy that everybody claims to favor, including their worst enemies. As an economist with a classical liberal perspective (the original perspective among economists, which is now resurgent), I believe that the nature of freedom can be clarified by beginning with some fundamental characteristics of social organization and of human ontology.

THE NATURE OF SOCIAL ORGANIZATION

While it is certainly true that human beings vary in their social inclination, as in all other human traits, the vast majority choose to associate with others in an interconnected group life, usually retaining, however, varying degrees of privacy. The most conspicuous and essential feature of this social interaction is technical, occupational specialization by the different individuals in a social division of labor. In and of itself, such a division of the socially useful and productive tasks and activities among the different members of society almost defines what it means to have a social organization.

The division of labor is productive, allowing increased physical output of goods and services and hence increased real incomes, which explains why people engage in it.[1] It is also inherently cooperative, and involves a great deal of trust, since each person, by being a specialist, is producing only a part of what he or she needs to survive, and relies on the rest to produce and supply the other things needed. Consequently, certain other social mechanisms must be present. First, there must be institutional mechanisms for allocating and reallocating (as needed) the available resources, land, people, and capital, across the specialties and occupations in the social division of labor (occasionally, even adding new specialties and deleting old ones), and for coordinating their activities. Also, there must be a social mechanism for product acquisition, so that people specializing in production can obtain the other things they need.

There are two archetypically opposite ways of organizing a society, with infinite shades of admixture. The first involves a hierarchical relationship among superiors and inferiors of various ranks and status. In the pure form of this kind of social and political structure, the coordination of activities, allocation of resources, and distribution of products is predetermined through central planning and issuance of orders by those at the top of the hierarchy for carrying out the plans. The orders are then enforced by the military and police. In the 20th century, the economic record of all nations with central planning systems was miserable. The story of Chile is that, in the early 1970s, it was rapidly being transformed into just such a system.

The alternative method is to organize society, as much as possible, around voluntary interactions between and among *equals*, with individual self-determination, and collective self-government in the form of minimal democratic political authority. In this structure, activities are coordinated, products are distributed and resources are allocated through individual decisions and mutually voluntary exchanges that both generate and are guided by market price, profit, and loss signals. This is what is properly termed as the free society, and it is in defining its parameters of individual choice and political constraint that the problem of defining freedom arises.

CHOICE UNDER CONSTRAINT

While there is a strong intuition to the notion that a person's freedom varies inversely with the constraints on what he or she can do or have, freedom as an attainable social condition cannot be defined as one in which there are no such limits. This is because no such condition can exist. Some constraints on what we can do are simply imposed by physical nature. The richest and most powerful person who had ever lived could not choose to be in two places at the same time or to escape the effects of gravity.[2] Other constraints are ontological (that is, conditions of our existence and nature as human beings). Most crucially, all human beings feel constrained by a condition economists call scarcity, in which the resources at their personal disposal are perceived as inadequate to allow them to attain, acquire, or accomplish all of their desired ends or goals. It is precisely this universal condition that forces individuals to rank their desired ends (that is, place them on a value scale) and allocate the limited available resources to the highest valued ends in the list, foregoing (at least temporarily) the rest. Assigning scarce resources to their most valuable uses is what it means to economize on their use.[3]

Crucially, it is only within the constraint of scarcity that we make choices, and it is, in part, the nature of freedom that it consists (to use Milton Friedman's famous phrase) in being free to choose. That is, *individual freedom consists in being free to choose and act on the basis of one's own value scale rather than being forced to do so on the basis of someone else's.* Notice, however, that this is not a sufficient definition of freedom as a general social and political condition, unless it applies to all persons equally (or at least to all adults), and making such a condition uniform itself implies some limit—some constraint—on personal choices and actions. In particular, a person may not morally and justifiably choose to forcibly impose his or her will on another adult, except in an act of self-defense, and may not choose to steal the goods or resources of another. Neither may a person take actions that negligently cause harm to others. Nearly all other choices and actions aimed at attaining personal well-being within the constraint of scarcity can be taken by the individual as a matter of right.[4]

There is another subtle but crucial point here. People can only attain their goals by applying available resources capable of satisfying those needs and desires, either directly, as consumer goods, or indirectly, in the form of productive assets capable of generating consumer goods. The most fundamental resources of all (of which, every person has one each) are the human mind and body. They can be employed to conceive what other resources are available or can be acquired, what ends are desirable, the steps by which such resources can be applied to attain the most desirable ends, and to carry out those steps. But to be free to choose and act to attain such goals for one's self necessarily implies the right to exclusive individual control over both one's self and at least some external resources. That is, it implies, in any social setting, private ownership of property that has been acquired by legitimate means.[5]

Freedom as a social and political condition exists, then, when people are allowed to privately own property and are constrained from killing, compelling, stealing from, or negligently harming each other. Individuals are otherwise free to choose and act for themselves, and the only remaining option for their interactions with each other is to do so in an open, honest, and mutually voluntary basis. That is, they must interact on the basis of open voluntary contract rather than of coercion or deception.

Economists have long since shown that in the nature of such mutually voluntary interactions, the well-being of both parties is increased. In a voluntary exchange transaction, for example, each party wants what they are trading *for* more than what they are trading *away* to the other party. Absent deception in the nature or quality of the goods, services, or assets, each party is made better off by the exchange in their own opinion. The same is true of other mutually voluntary interactions, including even acts of voluntary charity. This purely logical reasoning is buttressed by the historical fact that those nations that first began orienting their societies primarily around voluntary contract were the first to experience industrial revolutions and sustained economic growth with rising per capita real incomes.[6]

That historical experience is ongoing. More than a few nations in the late 20th century, including Chile, have escaped third-world poverty and entered the ranks of the prosperous nations. Others are hot on their heels.[7] All of these rapidly prospering nations have done so by adopting, to varying degrees, private property, open internal, and external markets, and the other cultural attitudes and institutional features of a free society. Massive empirical evidence shows both the material prosperity and the economic growth of nations to be positively correlated with the degree of their economic freedom.[8]

INTERNAL AND EXTERNAL CONSTRAINTS

The primary constraints necessary to prevent people from violating each other's rights and thus maintain the social condition of freedom are worth discussing. Four types seem central. The first, and most important, consists simply of personal moral inhibitions against violating the rights of others. Crucial here is simple honesty and respect for the persons and property of others, and tolerance for the right of others to have and to act on values different than one's own, as long as such actions are not predatory. These and related moral attitudes are crucial. If they are widespread, predation will be minimal, both because people acting on such internal values will not violate others' rights, and because they will apply informal social pressures (perhaps including ostracism) to those who do. Little in the way of other constraints will then be necessary to further suppress the remaining predation.

A second set of constraints on predatory behavior is economic in nature. Market competition, allowing consumers to substitute between independent suppliers of a good or service, for example, is an extremely potent social control mechanism tending to promote civility, product quality, and honest treatment of customers. Each competitor knows that customers must be *enticed*, and those who do not feel well treated will quickly switch suppliers. This incentive applies in both product and input (including labor) markets. Personal reputation, which must be maintained to allow future personal gains from exchange with others, is a crucial incentive for people to be reasonable, courteous, and live up to their commitments. Such social mechanisms obviously do not suppress all predation whether coercive or stealthy, but predatory activities would certainly be much larger in scope in their absence.

A third important set of constraints on predation consists of legal penalties. This is the realm of government, which properly exists, in the famous statement of the American Declaration of Independence, precisely to protect people's natural rights, thus maintaining a condition of voluntary interaction among equals, and must properly derive its just power from the consent of the governed. The government not only properly inhibits predatory activities by threat and application of punishment, but clearly defines and specifies the prohibited forms of behavior through legislation. In addition, it provides for due process of the law through which guilt or innocence of those accused is determined, contracts are enforced, and legal disputes settled. Add national defense and property registration (including patents and copyrights), along with the minimal taxation necessary to fund these few activities, and the list of legitimate governmental functions is virtually complete. Thomas Jefferson stated this perspective concisely:

> A wise and frugal government, which shall restrain men from injuring one another, which shall leave them otherwise free to regulate their own pursuits of industry and improvement, and shall not take from the mouth of labor the bread it has earned. This is the sum of good government. [9]

The necessity of having a government to restrain private coercion and theft through threat or application of legal penalties, and to provide the context of law and property rights protection in which the economic constraints can operate, raises the necessity of a fourth set of constraints on predatory activities. In the classical liberal scheme, government is properly created and its form and structure defined by a social contract (constitution) and is operated by agents elected from among the people themselves. Legal agents can only exercise powers specifically contractually granted by their principals. This fourth set therefore consists of constitutional constraints limiting the exercise of governmental power to its few legitimate functions, thus preventing government itself from becoming a tool through which some citizens oppress, coerce, or steal from others.

Constitutional requirement of periodic competitive elections for discrete terms of office, so that those who abuse governmental power may be removed, is one such social control mechanism. Another is constitutional division of authority among, and checks and balances between, the executive, legislative, and judicial branches, to prevent excessive power from accruing in any single set of hands. Most important, however, since majorities of voters may sometimes gain a desire to exploit unpopular individuals or minority groups (such as the currently wealthy), is that there be clear prescriptive and proscriptive constitutional limits on the decision making authority of even democratically elected officials, to prevent them from abridging individual rights.

William E. Simon, Treasury Secretary during the Nixon and Ford Administrations, once cogently observed that freedom is not a presence, but an absence—an absence of governmental constraint.[10] Had he added, "beyond that necessary to keep people from violating each other's rights," he would have had it just right. But that absence of governmental constraint can only be attained and maintained by subjecting government itself to a higher law that strictly precludes it from engaging in anything other than its legitimate protective functions. This condition in which government officials, even when operating at the public will, are themselves constrained by a higher law (the constitution) from making laws and/or exercising power in ways that reduce freedom and individual rights, is essentially what it means to have the rule of law, not of men.

IS WEALTH FREEDOM?

It is to be noticed that the definition of freedom developed here, in which people are left free to choose how to use their own scarce resources on the basis of their own values, and are otherwise constrained (by moral, economic, and legal pressures) only from violating the same rights of others, is invariant to the amount of wealth or real income any person has. It is certainly true that a poor person, who by definition possesses few assets, has far fewer effective options at a given point in time than does a rich person, who possesses more resources. Scarcity is much more constraining for the poor person, but they both have exactly the same freedom to choose and act for themselves within the constraints they face.

Nearly all opponents of the free society, however, equate freedom with income or wealth.[11] A claim is easy to make, and appears intuitional, that the poor person is not particularly free, being highly constrained in the options he or she has. From this perspective in which only "freedom from want" counts, equalizing freedom means equalizing income and wealth. The intent of the advocates of this view is precisely to accumulate the political power necessary to forcibly redistribute other people's incomes and wealth at will.

The confusion involved in failing to distinguish between the freedom to choose how to use one's own resources on the one hand, and the amount of resources one has on the other, should be obvious. It is also tragic, for some reasons that should, on reflection, also be obvious. First, in a free society, one of the options *always* available for a person's current resources, even if they are highly limited, is to employ at least part of them in ways that increase the resources available to that person over time. That is, part of one's time and energy can be spent in productive thought and labor, and part of one's available income and assets can be saved and invested or employed in ways that cause one's income, wealth, or human capital (knowledge and skills) to grow over time.[12] If this were not so, men and societies could never have become wealth, since not long back, historically speaking, virtually everyone, everywhere on earth was poor.[13]

The tragedy is, that engaging in government redistributions of wealth or income, in its nature, nearly always reduces the incentives people have to undertake such wealth and income generating actions. This is true both of those who are already more wealthy, who are taxed to provide the subsidies, and of those who are initially comparatively poor, who receive them. Typically, as both a theoretical and empirical matter, both groups will work, save, and invest less than they otherwise would have. Both the particular individuals involved and society at large end up poorer over time than they otherwise would be and *thereby less free than they otherwise would be by the very standard of those who equate the degree of people's freedom with the magnitude of their real incomes.*[14]

THE IRRITATIONS OF FREEDOM

One more thing that freedom is *not* deserves stress: a free society is *not* a utopia. While the evidence is overwhelming that people in freer societies tend to be come both wealthier and happier on average than those in less free societies, there are in fact many sources of discontent associated directly with the condition of freedom. As a condition in which people are constrained from violating each other's rights, for example, people who highly value such predatory actions will themselves feel highly constrained. There is little in human history that can be understood if it is not grasped that there are more than a few people who get satisfaction from dominating, coercing, and compelling others. Such people will be endlessly frustrated in a free society, and some of them will work very hard and long to remove the institutional and attitudinal constraints on the accumulation and exercise of arbitrary political power.

Another source of discontent inherent in the condition of freedom is the personal responsibility it necessarily imposes on people. When a person is free to choose and act for him or her self in some area of life, then by definition he or she is responsible for the consequences of the choices made (having generated them), whether those consequences are good or bad. Now the maximum incentive to make good choices about how one's time, energy, and other resources are to be used, and to avoid making bad ones, exists when the bulk of such consequences are experienced by the person making the choices. This is precisely the case under the condition of personal and social freedom. True, if one does something productive and provides goods or services on the market that others value highly, those others benefit, but they compensate that individual in exchange. On the other hand, one who uses resources inefficiently, or supplies goods or services on the market that others value less than their cost, suffers personal losses. This condition of personal responsibility and bearing of consequences under the regime of private ownership and voluntary exchange is precisely what generates overall productive and efficient resource use, and reliable economic growth with rising real incomes.

The problem here, for *some* people, is that personal responsibility is felt as a burden more than as an opportunity. Present choices and actions aimed at attaining future well-being always occur under uncertainty. Even with the best of intentions and judgment, mistakes can be made. More than a few people yearn to be relieved of these risks and burdens. Freedom in the minds of such people means freedom from the personal responsibility for, and consequences of, their own actions. They wish to have the downside risks socialized, so that others are compelled to bear the costs of their mistakes. Worse, they may even wish to be relieved altogether of the burden of choice by having others make their decisions and take care of them.

It either does not occur to such persons, or they do not care, that socialization of risks subsidizes bad resource use decisions, making society as a whole worse off than it would otherwise be. Nor do they care that such policies degrade the legitimate freedom of others. It is a profoundly important insight, for understanding the tyranny and poverty so many nations remain mired in to this day, and the marginal decline of freedom that has occurred even in America, to see the natural coalition between this group of people and the first group discussed above; between those who wish to control and dominate others, and those who wish others to make their decisions for them. *This coalition is naturally in opposition to those who wish to be free.*

Other sources of irritation in the free society are easy to find. Scarcity, though greatly relieved over time in such a society, will still be felt at any point in time. No matter how many of our desires we succeed in satisfying, it is always far easier to add more wants or larger projects to our list than it is to obtain the additional resources necessary to finance or otherwise obtain them. So we still feel constrained at the margin. Many are inclined to blame such constraint on others, notably the capitalist businessmen who supply them with goods, inevitably (given the reality of scarcity), at a cost.

In addition, it is an irritating feature of the very free and mutually beneficial exchanges through which we obtain our incomes, and with them the goods and services we desire, that how *much* we are able to obtain depends on the value *other* people place on *our* goods or productive services. Which of us is not inclined to feel that we are undervalued in the market? It is natural and easy to transfer this feeling into a resentment of the market itself. The enemies of freedom encourage such thinking.

Life appears to have inherent dissatisfactions, then, even in a free society. Perhaps this is as it should be, since without a feeling that conditions are less than perfect and could be improved upon, all efforts at progress would stop. The problem is, how such feelings of dissatisfaction can be prevented from expressing themselves in ways that destroy the free society that also seems to be a necessary condition for meaningful human well-being and progress.[15] In the case of Chile, tragically, it took a *military liberator* to accomplish this.

NOTES

1. This economic view that social organization and interaction is motivated by rational recognition of the potential resulting gains in productivity, real income, and personal well-being, contrasts starkly with the widespread sociological view that humans are simply driven by some innate internal biological or psychological impulse to associate. The sources of these productivity and real income gains in comparative cost advantages and differential preference rankings rooted in human individuality and geographical resource diversity are well understood by economists.

2. The possibilities of flight, orbit, or even of escape from a gravity well, do not imply escape from the effects of gravity. Physicists have shown that the speed and vector of an object under thrust sufficient to accomplish any of those things will be different than it would be absent the earth's mass and gravity by precisely the effect of the *presence* of the earth's mass and gravity.

3. It was with the publication of Lionel Robbins' *An Essay On the Nature and Significance of Economic Science* (London: Macmillan & Co., 1932) that scarcity, choice, and resource allocation, came to be recognized as the central organizing concepts of modern neoclassical economics.

4. The philosopher and novelist Ayn Rand correctly defined rights as morally legitimate freedoms to act in a social context. To discuss morally legitimate freedoms to act is therefore to discuss rights. See Rand, "Man's Rights," in *Capitalism: The Unknown Ideal*, ed. Ayn Rand (New York: Signet Books, 1967), 320–328.

5. More detailed discussion on the vital importance of the conceptual and institutional development of property rights to the advance of civilization is contained in the section on water law reform in Chapter 5 below.

6. See Nathan Rosenberg and L. E. Birdzell, Jr., *How the West Grew Rich: The Economic Transformation of the Industrial World* (New York: Basic Books, 1986).

7. See Leszec Balcerowicz and Stanley Fisher, *Living Standards and the Wealth of Nations: Successes and Failures in Real Convergence* (Cambridge, MA: MIT Press, 2006).

8. See James Gwartney, et al., *Economic Freedom of the World* (Vancouver, BC: Fraser Institute, 2004), and Steven T. Easton and Michael Walker, "Income, Growth, and Economic Freedom," *The American Economic Review* 87 (May 1997), 328–332.

9. President Jefferson's first inaugural address, 1801.

10. William E. Simon, *A Time for Truth* (New York: McGraw-Hill, 1978), 19.

11. See, for example, Amy Gutman, *Liberal Equality* (Cambridge, MA: Cambridge University Press, 1980): 8, and Robert Goodin, *Reasons for Welfare* (Princeton, NJ: Princeton University Press, 1988), 313.

12. For an illuminating personal example of this process under conditions of poverty, see *The Autobiography of Benjamin Franklin* (Clearwater, FL: Touchstone Books, 1997).

13. In 1890, by the modern, post World War II defined poverty level of real income, about 90 percent of the U.S. population was poor according to William Fogel, *The Fourth Great Awakening and the Future of Egalitarianism* (Chicago: University of Chicago Press, 2000), 170. Yet they did not starve, and indeed, were not only already prosperous by the world standards of the day, but were able to save, invest, innovate, and generate rapid economic growth.

14. The necessary condition for rising real *incomes* per hour is rising *output* per hour. Of all the social pathologies that were associated with the period of expanding income transfers in America beginning in the late 1960s, the one that worried economists the most was the decline in productivity growth below its historic two percent average annual rate after 1972. See James Rolph Edwards, *Regulation, the Constitution, and the Economy* (Lanham, MD: University Press of America, 1998), 173–179.

15. For massive documentation of the ongoing improvements in human life wrought by modern free societies, not just in those nations but worldwide, see Indur M. Goklany, *The Improving State of the World* (Washington, DC: The Cato Institute, 2007), and/or Julian Simon, *The State of Humanity* (Malden, MA: Blackwell Publishers, 1997).

Chapter One

Geography and Political History

One of the most amazing—and, in some respects, tragic—stories of the late 20th century concerns how the nation of Chile finally became a free society. Lying west of the Andean mountain chain and running along the coast all the way from Peru and Bolivia on the North down to the southernmost tip of South America, Chile is blessed with great mineral wealth, particularly copper, gold, silver, and nitrates. In the 19th and 20th centuries, copper and nitrates became enormously important mining industries and sources of export income. As the world industrialized, telephone and electrical systems using copper wire expanded, and fertilizer became an important input in agriculture everywhere. Chile was also blessed with good ports through which to ship its minerals and other exports, where cities such as Antofagasta, Valparaiso, and Concepcion grew. However, by far its biggest city, Santiago, was established in the interior of the Central Valley, between the Andes and the coastal mountain range.[1]

Like many other Latin American nations, as a result of the Spanish conquest, Chile was cursed with a semi-feudal social and economic structure. A small elite of large landholders exercised great control over a rural peasantry that was supplemented over centuries by the slave labor of conquered and captured Indians. These conditions, and the social stresses and conflicts they engendered, persisted long after Chile obtained its independence in 1825. Social conflict in Chile was not much ameliorated by growth in the mining industries at the turn of the 19th and 20th centuries. Mine workers were *not* forced out of the agricultural sector, but *drawn* out by the offer of *higher* wages by the mining firms than those so attracted could earn in Hacienda employment. Social conflict may have worsened, if anything, as mine workers increasingly unionized and a series of parliamentary governments extended the franchise.

Beginning in the 1930s, Chile enjoyed a long series of democratic governments with peaceful transitions of power. However, those governments, like many Latin American governments, followed deliberate policies of "import substitution." That is, they placed high tariffs on foreign manufactured imports, and often deliberately *undervalued* the Chilean currency on foreign exchange markets. This made foreign imports, particularly of manufactured goods, artificially expensive to Chileans and Chilean manufactured goods cheap in other nations. Import substitution was intended to encourage the growth of domestic manufacturing industries.

Those industries did indeed expand over time, as resources were redirected away from what were actually more productive and valuable uses. Thus, a large number of Chileans were drawn from agriculture into urban industrial employment. Following the lead of the mine-workers, many of those manufacturing workers unionized and mobilized for political action. At the same time, the relative decline in the nation's agricultural labor force strengthened the movement for unionization of agricultural employees, despite heavy resistance from the landowners.

Chilean society became increasingly politicized. Power shifted marginally away from the landowners and the industrialists, who had by then together come to constitute the conservative elite. Various organized groups and parties struggled to influence the legislative and executive authorities of the state to either coercively redistribute property and income *to them* (a process economists term *rent-seeking*), or to resist such redistribution *from* them by others. This diversion of scarce resources from *productive* investments into campaign contributions, lobbying, bribery, and so on, in ongoing efforts to influence politicians, added to the effect of import substitution and other bad policies in slowing the improvement in Chilean economic well-being.[2]

The ruling parties played these rent-seeking interest groups off against one another in competitive struggles to form winning electoral coalitions and in formulating policies. Socialist groups arguing for government takeover of the means of production and equalization of incomes progressively gained strength, and successive governments began nationalizing business firms. The bureaucracy expanded, making government employment a large fraction of all employment. The bureaucrats came to comprise the bulk of what constituted the middle class in Chile, and became a strong voting bloc and interest group applying pressure for ongoing government expansion at the expense of the private sector.[3]

What little understanding of the classical liberal principles of a free society that may have existed in Chile in earlier decades almost disappeared in this period, expect for its democratic component, which thrived in a perverted majoritarian form. By the 1950s, political and ideological discourse in Chile extended only from moderate business interventionism and democratic socialism in the middle, to Marxist communism on the extreme left.[4] Rising government expenditures were often financed by debt monetization through the Chilean central bank, resulting in both chronic and accelerating inflation. With all of this government resource misallocation, bureaucratization, inflation, and diversion of private resources into political rent-seeking, it is not surprising that Chile remained very poor, with one of the lowest rates of economic growth among Latin nations.[5]

CHRISTIAN SOCIALISM

In 1964, Eduardo Frei Montalva, candidate of the Christian Democrat Party, was elected Chilean President. The relatively new Christian Democratic Party (PDC), which had begun only in 1957, was essentially a democratic socialist party inspired by Catholic social doctrines. However, most of its members eschewed outright communism because of the increasingly anticommunist attitudes of the Catholic Church.[6] Frei defeated his Marxist opposition with aid from the U.S. government and from many voters from parties on the Chilean right who saw that their own party candidates had no chance of winning. Additional victory in the congressional elections of 1965 gave the PDC control over the Chamber of Deputies.

The Frei program of 'Revolution in Liberty' (*Revolucion en Libertad*) was not moderate, however, but radical even by prior Chilean standards. It aimed at industrial nationalization, redistribution of income, wealth, and land, and the extension of democratic political control and decision making to virtually every aspect of Chilean life and society.[7] Large scale confiscation of landed estates for redistribution to peasants began, the owners being compensated with thirty-year government bonds. After 1967, firms in the copper and other mining industries also began being nationalized.

In addition, the Christian Democrat government put enormous effort into organizing agricultural unions, radical student groups, and other groups aimed at agitating and lobbying for their conception of "social justice."[8] This greatly extended the politicization and radicalization of Chilean society. All this, of course, angered those on the right who had supported Frei in 1964. The representatives elected by the right therefore did what they could to obstruct the legislative agenda of the Frei government.

The Frei program ended up alienating not only the Chilean business (both large and small) and landed interests, but also many on the radical left. The latter actually saw the redistribution as too small and too slow, and were also irritated because the Frei government maintained good relations with the U.S. and with international lending agencies.[9] Investments in Chile by multinational corporations actually increased under the Frei government. Also, the radicalization and politicization of so many elements of Chilean society by the PDC seems to have taken on a life of its own, frightening and alienating other voters. Thus, the Christian Democrats began losing much of their support.[10]

SLIDING INTO COMMUNISM

In 1970, a coalition of radical left parties known as the *Unidad Popular* (Popular Unity, or UP) formed around Salvador Allende Gossens to oppose the Christian Democrats and the parties of the right. Allende, born in Valparaiso in 1908 and trained as a medical doctor, had helped found the socialist party of Chile in 1933 and had become its chairman. He served several terms in the Senate, and became Senate President in 1966. Allende was a dedicated Marxist, a friend of Fidel Castro and an open admirer of Soviet communism with close ties to the Chilean communist party. He had previously run for the Presidency of Chile in 1952, 1958, and 1964. Although he lost each time, in 1958 he came close enough to winning to frighten officials in the U.S. government.[11]

In 1970, Allende squeaked out a narrow plurality over the other candidates with 36.2 percent of the vote, despite the fact (made public later) that International Telephone and Telegraph, which owned 70 percent of Chitelco, the Chilean telephone and telegraph company, had given $700,000 to help elect Jorge Allesandri, the Conservative candidate. The Mitrokhin Archives, smuggled by KGB archivist Vasily Mitrokhin out of Russia and delivered to British Intelligence in 1992, however, show that the KGB had given Allende $400,000 for his electoral effort, and another $50,000 personally.[12] These outside efforts to affect the 1970 election largely canceled one another, and there is no one to whom to assign the credit or blame for Allende's plurality election but a large minority of Chilean voters.

Chilean politics being fragmented, with multiple parties and frequent plurality presidential election winners with consequent coalition governments, the tradition (occasionally violated) had long been that the candidate attaining the plurality became President. This time it took intense negotiations between UP and the Christian Democrats. In an omen of things to come, groups of Chilean women wearing black gathered to demonstrate outside La Moneda, the presidential palace in Santiago, and gave a letter with 20,000 signatures to outgoing President Frei begging him not to give the country away to communism.[13]

The negotiations between the UP and the PDC were further complicated when, a month after the election, the commander of the Chilean army, General Rene Schneider, was wounded in a botched kidnap attempt and died a few days later. Some believed that this attempted kidnapping was supported by the American CIA, with the expressed consent of Henry Kissinger, though he later denied it. The apparent intent was for the kidnapping to be blamed on

Chilean communists and weaken Allende. [14] Having failed, the result was the opposite. Threat of a military takeover evaporated for a time, and after signing a statute of constitutional guarantees to gain Christian Democrat support, Allende became the Chilean President.

Allende quickly undertook a program of industrial property confiscations, nationalization of Chilean banks, income redistribution, and land seizures on a scale that put the efforts of the previous Frei government to shame. The assets of several American companies, including Firestone, International Telephone and Telegraph, and Dow Chemical, were also expropriated. In 1939 the Chilean government had created CORFO (*Corporacion de Fomento de la Producion*), a huge holding company, to run its state-owned enterprises. According to Sebastion and Alexandria Cox Edwards, in 1970, when Allende was elected, CORFO controlled forty-six firms, none of which were financial firms. By 1973, it controlled 488 non-financial firms plus nineteen banks. [15] In late 1974 it owned 600 firms accounting for 40 percent of Gross Domestic Product (GDP). On top of that, the Allende government allowed many firms that were *not* nationalized to be illegally seized by unions or worker collectives. [16]

Allende also nationalized the health and education systems and established public works programs to provide employment for the poor. These massive expenditures generated huge budget deficits, reaching 10.7 percent of GDP in 1971 and growing to 30.5 percent of GDP in 1973. [17] The deficits were partly financed by central bank purchases of government debt (debt monetization) with newly created base money. In a futile attempt to limit the resulting price increases. Allende imposed price ceilings on goods and services in 1972 and 1973. [18] To be fair, as Chilean politics and thinking had moved left over time, price controls had been a part of Chilean life under several prior administrations, but Allende greatly extended them and enforced them stringently. [19]

Controls were also extended on foreign imports under Allende, isolating the economy even more than previously from world markets. Indeed, the whole foreign trade sector was virtually nationalized. Nearly the only imports allowed were government purchases, and the Chilean currency was *overvalued* by the administration to make such purchases cheap. This generated an international payments deficit that the government had to finance using previously accumulated foreign exchange reserves. [20] In addition, prior limits on capital account transactions (international transactions in bonds, corporate stocks, and credit) were made even more stringent. Ideologically, the stated motive of all this was to shut out and reduce the influence of the hated "foreign capital" and multinational corporations. Underneath this was an intent of the government to shut off the escape of wealth, as many domestic businessmen, faced with expropriation, tried to salvage what they could by investing abroad or purchasing foreign currencies that were *undervalued* by the governmentally fixed exchange rates.[21]

At first, the stimulus of Allende's monetary expansion combined with highly favorable copper prices on the world market, seemed to make all of this work. Chilean real GDP rose over eight percent in 1971, the Allende administration's first year, and unemployment fell to only four percent of the labor force, due to the vast expansion of employment in the bureaucracy.[22] In addition, these policies somewhat flattened the income distribution. Over the next two years, however, the economy began collapsing into chaos. The combination of rapid monetary expansion with price controls, as elementary economic theory would predict, generated huge shortages of goods and services and pervasive black markets, particularly for flour, rice, sugar, and beans.

The Allende administration had to import food and institute a food rationing program. Tens of thousands of Chilean mothers, known as *Momasinas*, went out into the streets of Santiago and other cities banging on pots and pans at 10 PM each night to protest the disappearance of basic commodities from the stores. Attacks on the *Momasinas* by leftist groups led to over a hundred injuries, and the UP government shut down three radio stations and a newspaper that supported them.[23] A hundred thousand *Momasinas* congregated at *Plaza de la Constitucion* in late August to express their frustration, and were dispersed with tear gas.[24] The government had to import food in large quantities, worsening the trade deficit. The foreign exchange reserves of the Chilean central bank were soon exhausted and the trade deficit could no longer be financed.[25]

None of these deterred Allende from his efforts to essentially abolish the market as an allocation mechanism and replace it with a centrally planned socialist system. The government established a system of networked telex machines and computers (Project Cybersyn) developed by British cyberneticist Stafford Beer to allow centralized economic planning in real time.[26] As any reader of Ludwig von Mises or Friedrich Hayek would expect, it did not work. In the absence of market determined prices for inputs and outputs necessary for rational cost calculations, and with a combination of bureaucratic and worker collective decision makers, all of whom lacked profit and loss incentives to operate efficiently, rational resource allocation and use were impossible to achieve.[27] The burden of nationalization, bureaucratization, arbitrary price ceilings, and resources misallocation was crushing to domestic production and commerce.

Government efforts to collectivize agriculture through various experiments that involved organizing confiscated land into collective farms, state farms, and so on, made conditions even worse. In fact, all these efforts *disorganized* production, as even Chilean intellectuals of the left now admit.[28] Agricultural output per capita declined in every year that Allende was

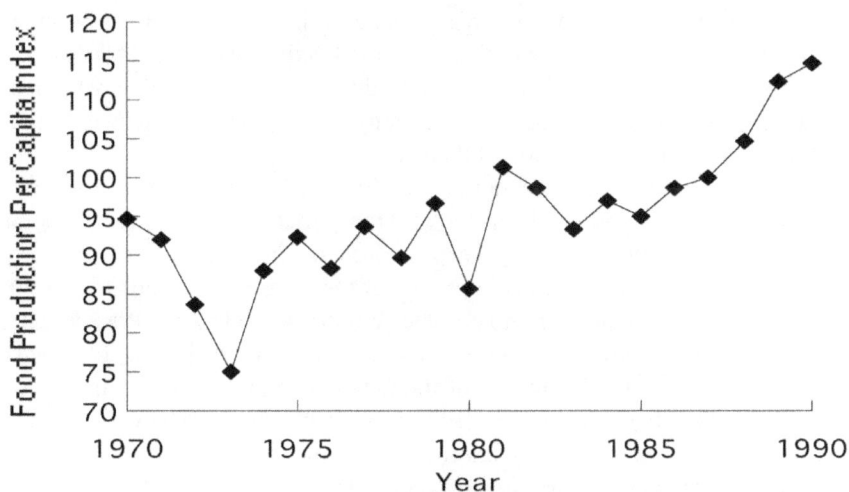

Figure 1.1. Per Capita Food Production, 1970-1990. Data Source: World Bank, World Tables, 1992.

in office, as Figure 1.1 shows. Rather than imposing order and rationality, the effort of the Allende government to collectivize assets, establish central planning, and abolish the market as the primary mechanism of price determination and resource allocation was literally destroying orderly social cooperation in every sector.

Seeing these things, and sensing where it was all headed, opposition to Allende grew rapidly, and a crisis approached. The revolt of the *Momasinas* was a big shock to the Allende government, since their actions were largely spontaneous. A wave of strikes began in October of 1972, first by truckers, then by small businessmen, several unions, student groups, and professionals, including medical doctors, to Allende's embarrassment. To make their strikes more effective these groups sought and obtained financial support from sympathetic social democratic parties in several European nations, from the American Federation of Labor and Congress of Industrial Organizations, and even from the CIA. Subsidies, loans, and other forms of aid for the Allende government poured in from Russia (usually funneled through the KGB) and from sympathetic East European communist governments.

Inflation was also an important factor stimulating this working class resistance. The Allende government had mandated several nationwide wage increases to solidify labor support, and the real wage rose by 17 percent in 1971. However, the rapid money growth necessary to finance government expenditures in 1972 and 1973 caused price increases to exceed subsequent wage increases, reducing the real wage in both of those years. The food shortages generated by the price controls also worsened the conditions. Even some labor groups initially very sympathetic to the UP government became unhappy. The representatives of the worker collectives which had taken over many private firms were often ignored by the government officials who had ultimate power. For all these reasons, many workers began organized protests *against* the nationalization of their firms.

Desperate at the near economic paralysis generated by the truckers' strike, Allende ordered his Minister of Transportation, Jamie Favovich, to begin requisitioning trucks to keep goods moving. When the truckers planned further demonstrations in protest of the government plans to form a state-owned transportation company, the administration had the President of the Chilean Truck-Owners Confederation, Leon Vilarin, jailed. Truckers, recognizing this as the beginning of the nationalization of truck transportation, demanded that Favovich be fired, and went to court. The Chilean appeals court declared the confiscation of private trucks unlawful and ordered the UP government to return them to their owners.[29] In further actions, Chilean courts declared several other government takeovers to be unlawful and ordered the properties returned, but the Allende administration refused to obey.

On May 26, 1973, Chile's Supreme Court unanimously denounced the failure of the Allende government to obey its resolutions and decisions.[30] This event seems to have solidified much anti-Allende sentiment, bringing pressure on the Chilean military. Having long been self-consciously neutral and independent of politics, the Military became increasingly disenchanted with the Chilean political process, and was made more so by the actions of the UP government. As the political situation deteriorated, Allende appointed several military generals to important government positions, most importantly army General Carlos Prats, in hopes of forestalling a coup. Many wives and daughters of the military officers joined the *Momasinas* in opposition to this, however, and shamed their husbands and fathers for their apparent co-option by the UP.[31] The officers reluctantly began to rethink their neutrality.

In late June, there was an abortive coup attempt by Colonel Roberto Souper, commander of a tank regiment, which temporarily surrounded the President's official residence, *La Moneda*. The *tanquetazo* (tank putsch) was in a shambles from the first. As the convoy of tanks, armored cars, and troops headed from their barracks to the center of Santiago, it stopped at every traffic light and obeyed every traffic rule. Reports indicate that at least one tank stopped to gas up at a commercial station. The government was not in much better shape, however, as a key event indicated. The KGB was warned in advance of the Putsch, and informed Allende, who broadcasted an appeal for the people to come out in the streets and defend his government. They did not.[32] Nevertheless, this half-hearted coup quickly fizzled, suppressed by the

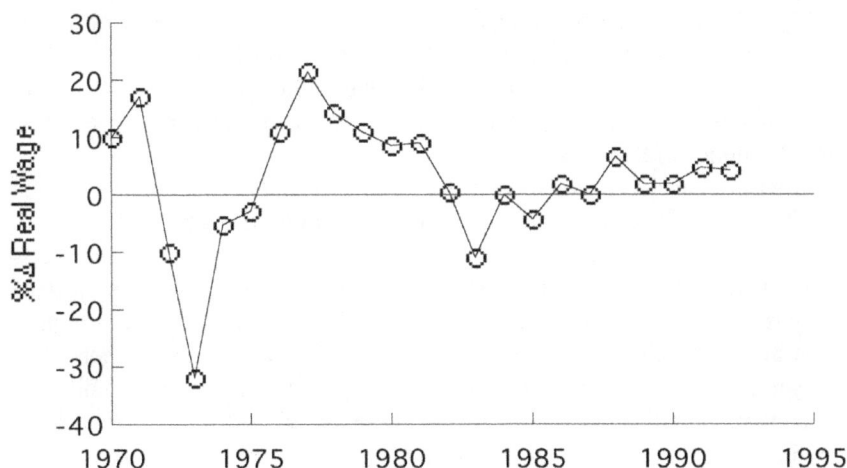

Figure 1.2. Annual Percent Changes in Real Wage. Data Source: Chilean Central Bank.

military itself at Allende's order. However, a general strike that followed early in July further signaled widespread public dissatisfaction.

Allende had lost the support of the Christian Democrats and many others in the Chilean Congress, and was acting by fiat. Unlike the Frei government, Allende's business confiscations were mostly without approval of the legislature, and the Chamber of Deputies passed several constitutional amendments that would have restricted the actions Allende was taking. On August 22, 1973, a majority of the Deputies—though less than the two-thirds required to *convict* the President of abuse of power—voted to openly censure Allende for acting unconstitutionally. In desperation, the deputies called upon the military to enforce constitutional government. Two of the three branches of government had now spoken.

The bill of particulars voted by the Deputies was damning. Among other things, it indicted Allende for ruling by decree, refusing to enforce judicial decisions, usurping control of the news media, illegally limiting emigration, and organizing and arming socialist militias to confront the military, all with intent to impose a totalitarian system. [33] Certainly, the Deputies were correct in that conclusion. The members of the administration, all of the members of the UP coalition, and others actively supporting its illegal and tyrannical actions were engaged in treasonous sedition.

All of the hallmarks of an incipient Soviet style totalitarian tyranny, including control of the media, mechanisms for preventing citizens from *leaving* the country, abolition of the market, and socialization of the economy, including a mechanism for central planning, were in place or in process. The

only thing needed to justify suspension of remaining civil liberties was sufficient crisis, and that was rapidly building. The day before the vote in the
Chamber of Deputies leftist radicals attacked a National Party demonstration
before Congress, injuring several people. That night they instituted a reign of
terrorist bombings and shootings in conservative middle and upper class
neighborhoods of Santiago.

Blaming the rising violence on the right, defenders of Allende claim that
all his "reforms" were in fact done peacefully, within the democratic process
and without violent coercion by the state. This claim only rises to the status
of a half-truth by ignoring the coercive character of the accelerating private
business nationalization, land confiscation, price controls and other regula-
tions of the remaining private sector. In fact, they were nothing more than
enormous gunpoint thefts at the hand of a collectivist administration directed
by a mere plurality President. All of these policies severely reduced the
freedom of Chileans, and most were undertaken by diktat. The only partial
truth in such apologetics is that Allende did not forcibly suppress the opposition parties. It was an open plan of the UP coalition, however, that the
Chilean Congress be abolished and replaced with a "people's assembly,"
which certainly would have consisted only of communist *apparatchicks*.

That had not been done by mid 1973 *only because Allende was not yet in
a position to do so*. He did not have the support of the Chilean military or of
the Caribineros (the national police force), and he had not yet built a sufficient force of armed socialist militias, though he was doing so as fast as he
could, using public funds created by the central bank along with money and
weapons supplied by both the Soviet KGB and Cuba.[34] Allende had already
reorganized his security service, the *Servicio de Investigationes* to intimidate
political enemies, and they had turned the cellars of their headquarters into
torture chambers.[35]

In late September, after the vote in the Chamber of Deputies, the military
found a Guerilla training camp with large stocks of weapons at Nehuentue in
rural southern Chile. Worse, it had recently discovered serious infiltration
into its ranks by leftist organizations. Many ranking military officers began
to realize that the deputies and the courts were right, and failure to act could
be fatal, both to them personally and for Chile as a nation. To reverse the
emerging communist tyranny and deflect the coming bloody suppression of
those opposed to that tyranny, someone with the power to do so and a belief
in freedom—a liberator—had to act.

NOTES

1. For a more complete description of Chile's geography, natural resource and industrial
pattern see the early chapters of Brian Loveman, *Chile: The Legacy of Hispanic Capitalism*,
3rd ed. (New York: Oxford University Press, 2001).

2. On the nature of rent-seeking and the social problem it generates, see the classic article by Gordon Tulloch, "The Welfare Costs of Tariffs, Monopoly, and Thefts," *Western Economic Journal* (June 1967): 224–232.

3. On all of these, see Andres Valesco, "The State and Economic Policy," in *The Chilean Economy: Policy Lessons and Challenges*, eds. Barry Bosworth, Rudiger Dornbusch, and Raúl Labaán, (Washington DC: The Brookings Institution, 1994): 379–429, particularly 380–382.

4. Juan Gabriel Valdez, *Pinochet's Economists: The Chicago School in Chile* (Cambridge: Cambridge University Press, 1995) is a good source for much of this history.

5. Valesco, 380, and Sebastian Edwards, "The Chilean Pension Reform: A Pioneering Program," in Martin Feldstein, *Privatizing Social Security* (Chicago, IL: University of Chicago Press, 1998); 33.

6. Loveman, 230-235.

7. Loveman, 237.

8. Valdez, 201-202, 236. See also Valesco, 392-393.

9. Loveman, 239.

10. See Valesco, 393-395, and Loveman, 240-243.

11. Loveman, 230.

12. Christopher Andrew and Vasili Mitrokhin, *The World Was Going Our Way: The KGB and the Battle for the Third World* (New York: Basic Books, 2005), 72.

13. Edy Kaufman, *Crisis in Allende's Chile: New Perspectives* (New York: Praeger, 1996), 65.

14. Mark Falcoff, "Kissinger and Chile," *Commentary Magazine* (10 November 2003). See also Loveman, 248.

15. Sebastian Edwards and Alejandra Cox Edwards, *Monetarism and Liberalization: The Chilean Experience* (Cambridge MA: Ballinger, 1987), 95-96.

16. Loveman, 251.

17. The World Bank, *World Tables 1992* (Washington DC: World Bank) for the 1971 observation; and Vittorio Corbo and Leonardo Hernandez, "Successes and Failures in Real Convergence: The Case of Chile," in *Living Standards and The Wealth of Nations*, eds. Leszek Balcerowicz and Stanley Fischer (Cambridge, MA: MIT Press, 2006): 120 (Table 5.1), for the 1973 and subsequent observations.

18. Edwards and Edwards, 7.

19. Vittorio Corbo and Stanley Fischer, "Lessons from the Chilean Stabilization and Recovery," in *The Chilean Economy, Policy Lessons and Challenges*, eds. Barry Bosworth, Rudiger Dornbush, and Raul Laban (Washington DC: The Brookings Institution, 1994), 35.

20. Edwards and Edwards, 6–9; Corbo and Fischer, 30, 34.

21. See Loveman, 250, on the capital flight by Chilean businessmen attempting to escape confiscation by the UP government.

22. Edwards and Edwards, 7.

23. Kaufman, 66.

24. Editorial, "The Bloody End of a Marxist Dream," *Time Magazine* (24 September 1973).

25. By the first quarter of 1973 international reserves held by the Chilean Central Bank had fallen to a level barely sufficient to finance two more months' worth of imports.

26. See Eden Medina, "Designing Freedom, Regulating a Nation: Socialist Cybernetics in Allende's Chile," *Journal of Latin American Studies* 38 (2006): 571–606.

27. See Ludwig Von Mises, *Human Action*, 3rd revised ed. (New York: Henry Regnery, 1966): 698–715.

28. Loveman, 250.

29. Kaufman, 74-82, 266-267.

30. "Salvadore Allende," *Wikipedia* (27 May 2009).

31. Kaufman, 67.

32. Andrew and Mitrokhin, 84.

33. "The 1973 Chilean Coup d'état," *Wikipedia* (8 September 2010); and Steve J. Stern, *Battling for Hearts and Minds: Memory Struggles in Pinochet's Chile*, 1971–1988 (Durham, NC: Duke University Press, 2006), 21–22.

34. "Bultos Cubanos," special ed., *Que Pasa* magazine (1982): 21; and Loveman, Op cit., 254.
35. Andrew and Mitrokhin, 82.

Chapter Two

Liberation Begins

As it turned out, the Chilean Congress and Supreme Court probably got more then they asked for. On September 11, 1973, the military, led by Augusto Pinochet Urgarte, who had recently been appointed Army commander by Allende himself, took action. *La Moneda* was shelled and assaulted by troops. The initially stiff resistance from Allende's 300 member elite Praetorian Guard (the GAP, or *Grupo de Amigos Personales*) led by Cuban-trained commando Ariel Fontana, eventually crumbled. Allende sat in a chair, put the barrel of an AK 47 under his chin and shot himself to death before he could be captured.[1]

With the fall of *La Moneda* and death of Allende, the army quickly began hunting Chilean communist militias and important socialist leaders. This aggressive action by the military seems to have caught most of the militant left by surprise and stifled much resistance, though not all. Fighting broke out in Concepcion between the Chilean military and groups of Allende's armed UP coalition supporters, which were not entirely suppressed until September 14th. Smaller scale violent conflicts between the security forces and armed radicals occurred throughout the provinces.

On the 12th, the day after the coup, the National Stadium of Chile was set up as a temporary detention center, and by the 22nd of September, about 7,000 leftists had been rounded up and detained there. Others were similarly held in other stadiums, perhaps totaling 40,000 altogether, until more permanent camps could be established to hold those believed to be centrally complicit in the seditious effort to communize Chile. The majority of the detainees were eventually released without further harm, but some of the worst leftist radicals were tortured for information and a few, including the folk singer Victor Jara, were taken and killed.

In October, apparently acting on intelligence already gathered, some seventy of the most influential communist revolutionary leaders were rounded up throughout the provinces, taken from their cells and summarily executed in what became known as the "Caravan of Death." The Caravan was led by General Sergio Arellano Stark. One of those killed in the Caravan was Comandante Pepe, who led 60 to 80 guerillas in an assault on a police station in the city of Neltume on September 12, right after he heard about the military coup. The Carabineros inside successfully held them off until help arrived, however.[2] Comandante Pepe was caught not long thereafter.

Fighting continued between armed communist groups and the military over the next several months. The Army suffered 34 casualties in the assault on *La Moneda* itself, killing 44 GAP fighters in the process. Another 116 Chilean soldiers were killed and injured in mop-up operations during September. In all, the army suffered 163 deaths in the first three months of military rule.[3] Adding in police casualties, as many as 756 servicemen and police are reported to have been killed or wounded in guerilla actions. Sympathetic leftists in other Latin nations aided the guerillas for years. In 1976, a plan to infiltrate 1,200 Marxist guerillas into Chile from Argentina was stifled by cooperation between Argentine and Chilean authorities.[4]

Pinochet and the other leaders of the coup quickly formed a military Junta to govern the nation, consisting of the top officers from the Chilean Army (Pinochet himself), Navy (Admiral Jose Toribo Merino Castro), Air Force (General Justavo Leigh Guzman), and the Caribineros (Director Cesar Mendoza Duran).

On October 13th, in one of its first political acts the Junta banned all political parties to the left of the Christian Democrats. Not long after that, and to the surprise of the remaining parties, they banned all organized political activity. Democracy was suspended for the duration of military rule, and nobody knew how long that would be. In December of the next year, after just a few months of joint rule, Pinochet was appointed President, and thereafter the other Junta members acted as a legislature.[5] They were not elected, of course, but they acted otherwise on democratic principles and agreed to strictly limit their own authority up front. A unanimous vote in favor, with President Pinochet concurring, was required in order to pass any legislative act.

As the military began raiding the various UP coalition party headquarters and rounding up as many of the leaders as they could find, they found many documents detailing plans and proposals in development for transforming Chile into a Leninist/Stalinist state. In the process they discovered how fortunate it was that they had acted when they did. On the desk of Allende's communist Undersecretary for the Interior was a document detailing "Plan Zeta" (or Plan Z) to murder the military high command at an upcoming Presidential banquet, then assassinate civilian opposition leaders to begin the final takeover. Other documents specified the locations of terrorist training camps and revealed plans for training and arming militias, coordinating militia assaults on police stations and military sites throughout the country in a takeover.

The military government released many of these documents to the media as they were found and analyzed. Similar documents also came from *Caribinero* and regional police units conducting raids on local radical-left groups. As these documents became public, many previously skeptical members of a shocked Chilean public were finally able to see the UP coalition intention of imposing communist tyranny that Allende and other UP leaders had previously been able to deny. This perception was strengthened when the government released what it called the *White Book* synthesizing all these plans, and as discoveries of arms caches quickly implicated all of the UP coalition parties.

It is probably true that the White Book overstated the integrated character of the UP coalition plans. All of the parties in the coalition were united in their intention to socialize Chile. As such they cooperated in that effort, though disagreeing in details of strategy. However, each of them wished ultimately to end up in charge, subordinating the others. One document even detailed a plan to kill Allende himself and replace him with a more forceful leader. Certainly, no tightly integrated takeover plan commissioned, formulated, or accepted by Allende would have contained such a provision.

The *White Book* also lacked sufficient documentation to prove some of its claims. Many scholars of the intellectual left have since, on the basis of such observations, been eager to dismiss the document releases and the White Book as a simple forgery and disinformation effort by the military government, and absolve everyone but the most radical communist elements within the UP coalition of any ill intent. In this strange view murderous intentions only existed on the part of the military and the conservative right segments in society. Only a negligibly few extreme leftists were so afflicted, and the UP government posed no real threat to Chilean democracy or freedom.[6] Given the long-standing tradition of moderation and political neutrality of the military in Chile, and the reluctance with which Pinochet and the other military leaders eventually undertook the coup, this perspective actually leaves no rational explanation for their actions during and subsequent to September 1973 beyond a sudden fit of institutional, sociopathic, paranoid psychosis.

Such arguments are unpersuasive given the undeniable authenticity of so many of the documents detailing plans in processes and the whole trend of policy during the Allende years including the known efforts of the UP to establish a "parallel" military, as well as the training camps and arms caches subsequently found. Even some repentant Chilean ex-communists such as Roberto Ampuero have since admitted publicly that Allende was trying to demolish Chilean democracy.[7] A key observation here is that as the crisis developed, nearly all international aid for the Allende government came from single-party communist dictatorships in the U.S.S.R. and from Cuba, with smaller amounts from Red China and North Korea. Financial support from the West European Social Democracies mostly went to the Christian Democrats and other *opponents* of the Allende regime. True *democratic* socialists everywhere knew what side Allende was really on, what his intentions were, and where his policies were going.

One should also recognize, with regard to the holes in the documentary evidence of the *White Book*, that the first thing conspirators do when faced with capture before their own murderous plans and organizational efforts are complete, is to *destroy as many incriminating documents as possible before going underground*. Massive document destructions occurred at all UP coalition party headquarters, and in some cases actually began in anticipation some days before the coup occurred. Only the swiftness with which the military moved once it overcame its reluctance resulted in as many documents being recovered as were.

Strenuous efforts by the Junta to suppress communists and other socialist radicals, finding, imprisoning, and sometimes killing them, continued for several years, though the worst brutalities occurred in the first few months. Official government reports issued in the 1990s, after democracy was restored, indicate that, over the whole period of the military government, as many as 2,279 people, who were referred to as "The Disappeared" because nobody claimed to know what had happened to them, were killed by the Junta's secret police. Perhaps another 20,000 Chileans were said to have gone into exile from fear of death, imprisonment, or torture if they stayed.

Some of those who fled were simply going home. To gain strength rapidly Allende had turned Chile into a haven for Marxist revolutionaries from all over Latin America. True, most of those fleeing were indigenous Chileans, but many from both groups left with intent to regroup, gain financing, weapons, and recruits, in order to return as more effective guerilla forces. In an effort to prevent this, Chile and other military governments in the region engaged in a joint effort known as Operation Condor, in which assassins were sent to kill the leaders of those groups. One of the persons targeted, Orlando Letelier, a former Chilean Ambassador to the U.S., was killed by a car bomb in Washington D.C. on 21 September 1976.[8]

All of these numbers are of debatable accuracy. Many of the "Disappeared" simply went underground. Others were wrongly labeled as "Disappeared" and were later found to be alive and well. Likewise, the Mitrokhin Archives show that the Soviet KGB acted with some success to exaggerate the atrocities committed by the Chilean government. For example, they forged a fictional letter from the head of DINA, the national police agency, to Pinochet, regarding the funding of efforts to assassinate Pinochet's enemies in Latin nations, the U.S., and Europe, then leaked the letter. It was accepted as genuine by major newspapers all over Western Europe and the U.S. Many of those looking into atrocities of the military government had incentives to exaggerate them. The report of the Rettig Commission on Truth and Reconciliation, established by the Alwyn government in 1990, was written by Raul Rettig, a longtime politician of the Radical Party, which was one of the major parties of the UP coalition. Still, when all is said and done, in the process of overthrowing Allende's incipient communist tyranny and struggling to defeat the partisans of that tyranny, it is not debatable that elements of the Chilean security forces felt compelled to commit many horrible acts, and did so.

The intellectual and political enemies of the Pinochet government have, of course, seized on its' intermittent violations of civil rights to characterize it as being dictatorial, murderous, and oppressive. Such claims are exaggerated, misleading, and lack context. Even if all of the official estimates of those killed are taken at face value and the losses of the security forces are added in, a startling fact emerges. *The death toll from the 1973-1990 Chilean liberation and pacification, seen either as a percent of population or in absolute numbers, was among the smallest in the entire history of Latin American Revolutions.*

Moreover, Latin America has often seen military takeovers establishing authoritarian dictatorships that changed nothing, and that ruled only for the sake of doing so. From the first, in contrast, the Chilean Junta sought an alternate vision of social, political, and economic organization as a guide for national reform, and was willing to look outside the normal spectrum of Chilean ideology and politics to fine it. They knew the old politics and thinking had led to disaster, and they wanted to find out what could work, and fast. It is precisely here that the story of Chile takes a twist, because, through an odd set of circumstances, events, and actions, a source of help was available.[9]

THE CHICAGO BOYS

American foreign aid agencies seldom do good, but in the early 1950s one called the International Cooperation Administration (which later became the Agency for International Development, or AID), did so. The ICA transferred a man named Albion Patterson to Chile where he was to provide advice for a local agricultural development program. From prior experience in other Latin countries Patterson had noticed and come to lament a general lack of economic knowledge and expertise in the region. Further, Patterson himself came to appreciate free-market economic thinking. According to leftist historian Juan Gabriel Valdez, who has interviewed many of the participants in these events, this happened because Theodore (Ted) Schultz, on leave from the University of Chicago where he was Chairman of the economics department, walked into Patterson's office one day and made his acquaintance. They became friends, and over time Schultz converted Patterson to Schultz' human capital theory of economic development.[10] Together they formulated a plan to persuade the ICA to arrange and at least partly fund a contract between a Chilean University and the University of Chicago to train native Chilean economists.

Patterson had success with his agricultural development program, and thereby impressed his superiors enough for them to green light his efforts to arrange such a contract. Schultz apparently had little trouble convincing his department colleagues and the administration at the University of Chicago. The thought of an influx of Latin students into their graduate school of economics was pleasant, and according to Valdez, Chicago economists were eager for an opportunity to oppose the influence in Latin America of the radical leftist views of Raul Prebish on economic development being propagated by the U.N. Economic Commission for Latin America. Plus, it was an opportunity to see whether they could actually stimulate economic development by increasing the human capital in Chile, specifically by training competent economists.[11]

At first they tried to interest the Chilean national university in Santiago (*Universidad de Chile*), but the leftist economists already there knew of the free-market reputation of the University of Chicago, and opposed any such project. In 1954, however, an official from the Catholic University in Santiago approached Patterson about help with its agricultural department. Patterson, seeing his opportunity, sold the man on his joint economics project instead. That was not an easy sell to other parties at either institution, however. Chicago school economists were leery of teaching at a religious university, and Catholic University officials were just as leery of a secular approach to human interactions that might conflict with Catholic social teachings. But both institutions eventually saw net gains from the deal. Catholic University had no economics program, and would likely gain prestige and attract students from association with the University of Chicago. So, they reached agreement. In 1955, the U.S. ambassador to Chile officially sanctioned the contract, to take effect in 1956 and run for three years. It was repeatedly extended.

The University of Chicago initially sent three economists to Catholic University, funded by a grant of $375,000 from the ICA. They established a rigorous program of undergraduate economics training, also offering a degree in business administration, which ended up attracting many more students than did the pure economics program. As excellent students emerged, they were invited to take a verbal interview for an opportunity to attend the University of Chicago for graduate training. Valdez admits that candidates actually came from *three* sources: the economics program at Catholic University, from its agronomy program, and from the Institute of Economics at

Universidad de Chile.[12] When these students came back from Chicago, many went to work for Chilean businesses, but some were hired at Catholic University. The first three hired there, according to Valdez, were Sergio de Castro, Luis A. Fuenzalida, and Pedro Jeftanovich. Others were added over time, and by the mid 1960s they were largely running the economics program themselves. It was these native, highly skilled Chilean economists with free-market leanings, in and outside of Catholic University, who became known as the "Chicago Boys."

The Chicago Boys did not have an easy time of it in Chile. The intellectual climate in the nation (and even in the rest of Catholic University) was hostile and for some time publication opportunities outside the university itself were few and far between. Their communications were mostly among themselves and with their students. Even the business community was not particularly supportive of their free-market views. Many members of that community favored the protectionist trade policies that successive Chilean governments had followed for so long, because they saw themselves as dependent on those policies. In addition, free-market views simply seemed strange to Chileans living at the time, few of whom had ever heard such a perspective.[13]

The climate began to change under Frei's Christian Democratic government. The conservative interests, who had largely supported Frei against the Marxist candidate, felt increasingly desperate as the Frei government became more radical, particularly after the combined electoral support of the conservative and liberal parties of the right declined severely in the 1965 congressional elections. Strong measures seemed in order, and the two parties of the right combined into the National Party.[14] Also, in 1968, many members of the Chilean business elite held a "National Convention of Production and Trade" designed to politically organize and unify businessmen and entrepreneurs.[15] That movement subsequently had significant success at slowing legislative enactment of radical Frei government programs.

The situation also seems to have motivated many among the large and small business, mining, and landed interests to undertake some serious rethinking of their own political and economic perspectives. Some, perhaps already influenced by the Chicago Boys who had gone to work for their firms, began to think seriously about the fundamental benefits of private property and free enterprise, and decided they needed to educate the Chilean public at large. A business group controlled by Augustin Edwards (no relation to the present author), who ran El Mercurio, among the most influential of all Chilean newspapers, hired several Catholic University economists in 1968 to write articles for an economic section in the paper. In addition, Augustin set up a think tank called The Center for Social and Economic Studies, to disseminate the free-market perspectives and principles of the Chicago Boys among people in the Business community.

Another factor that helped was the business success of some of the Chicago Boys themselves. Valdez reports that a Chicago Boy named Manuel Cruzat, who ardently wished to help save private enterprise in Chile, took over a private bank, fired many of its older executives, and brought his brother-in-law in to help him run the business. Together they bought into other business enterprises and ended up establishing one of the most important business groups in Chile. [16]

Another prime example is Sebastian Pinera who started out as an economics professor like his brother but then went into business. He was instrumental in introducing the use of credit cards in Chile in the late 1970s and invested his earnings in LAN Airlines. Later he became the owner of Chilevision, a television channel broadcasting nationwide, and to hold major shares in several other businesses, eventually obtaining a net worth of one billion in US dollars. [17]

On campus, however, things were going less smoothly for the Chicago Boys. Early in the Frei administration, the school of economics was pressured to add several left-wing economists to their faculty and expand their curriculum to add courses on Keynesian and even Marxist economics. [18] Another shock came in 1967 when student demonstrators radicalized and organized by the Christian Democrats took over many Chilean university campuses. Most university administrations caved in to their demands. At Catholic University, only the economics department was not occupied. These frightening events also seemed to have solidified the intent of the Chicago Boys and their students to reform Chilean society. They began by raising money from the business community and moving part of their operations to a separate campus. [19]

The situation continued to deteriorate, however, as Allende took power. In January of 1971 the post of Dean was eliminated and the school of economics was merged into an "Institute for Economics" headed by Eduardo Garcia, a left-wing Christian Democrat who had been Deputy Director of Planning in the Frei administration, although, as Valdez reports, every Chicago professor voted against him. The Chicago Boys still dominated the department intellectually, however, and before long were able to regain control of the school, forcing Garcia to quit and having him replaced with Jorge Cauas, a PDC economist more sympathetic to them. [20]

Valdez says that not long after Allende took over as President of Chile, some of the Chicago Boys, led by Sergio Underagga, began planning in earnest to change things. Having recognized early the fatal flaws of Allende's policies and publicly predicted the collapse to come, they began secretly working in August of 1971 to design their own program of reform that, if instituted, would not only reverse Allende's Marxist/Leninist policies, but establish, for the first time, a truly free society in Chile. According to

Valdez, some like-minded PDC economists were also brought in, expanding the group.[21]

Arnold Harburger, the famous microeconomist at the University of Chicago, whose wife was Chilean and who knew and mentored all the principals in these events, tells this story somewhat differently than Valdez. According to Harburger, the first systematic planning for Economic reform in Chile by the Chicago Boys actually occurred some years earlier at the request of *Frei* government officials, who found the resulting plan not to be to their taste. When Allende took over and began turning Chile into a Marxist-Leninist dictatorship, the Chicago Boys reconstituted their group and began revising their previous plan. The resulting brief document was called *El Laudrillo* (The Brick). Harburger attributes leadership of the planning group to Sergio De Castro and Hernan Buchi, and says that it included, among others, Juan Carlos Mendez, Sergio de la Caudra, Miguel Kast, and Jose Pinera.[22] In any case, their reform plan was worked out and ready before the military liberation even occurred.

A JUNTA IN SEARCH OF A POLICY?

Valdez says that when the Junta took control in 1973 it had the support of a vast transient coalition of political parties, trade unions, businessmen, landed interests, and other social groups, but that it lacked a coherent program for reform. He further claims that the Junta was initially undecided, however, in selecting between programs of restoration, in which a period of repressive pacification would provide a bridge to the next civilian administration, and one of foundation, involving an effort to transform Chilean mentality and institutions.[23]

The first claim is largely correct. In general, the Junta firmly intended from the first to reduce the role of government and increase the role of the private sector in the economy, and actually enunciated that intent in a formal "Declaration of Principles" in March of 1974.[24] However, they lacked clarity on many details and principles. The Chicago Boys provided much of that knowledge and clarity later. Valdez' second claim seems more dubious. First, the two programs—restoration and foundation—are not mutually exclusive alternatives. Second, the alleged dichotomy and indecision does not comport with the Junta's immediate and vigorous effort to physically remove the most radical members of the left from Chilian society.

Both this and later actions of the Pinochet government, to be discussed below, are better interpreted as indicating that the Junta decided early to follow a transformational course of action in which forceful pacification was seen as an initial element, necessary to establish a free society in Chile with a civilian, democratic government. An equally important initial set of measures was also necessary to deal with the existing economic crisis. Accordingly, while not entirely oblivious to existing interests, or unaware of the need for popular support and a source of claimed legitimacy for its power, the Junta quickly asserted its independence in economic policy making.

Valdez says the Navy commander was given initial charge of economic policy, and began approaching technical experts from the PDC (the Christian Democrats) to construct an economic team. Some declined, but other Christian Democrats such as Jorge Cauas and Raul Saez (who became the initial minister of Finance) signed on. However, the Navy—which according to Valdez loathed socialist views and leaned toward (classical) liberal policies—also contacted Hernan Cubillos, a member of the advisory board of *El Mercurio*, who recommended the Chicago Boys.[25] Jorge Cauas may also have recommended them, though it was not until 1975 that Sergio De Castro was hired as his subordinate, and many other Chicago Boys began being appointed to important positions.

Though they had to compete for control with the existing entrenched PDC economists and other policy advisers who often disagreed with them, the Chicago Boys had the advantage of having a reform plan ready that appealed to the transformational goals and aspirations of the military liberators. Accordingly, Chicago Boys were increasingly appointed to cabinet and other high level positions. Sergio de Castro himself became Economic Minister in April of 1975 and immediately began implementing elements of *El Ladrillo*. When he switched to being Finance Minister in December of 1976 he was replaced as Economic Minister by Pablo Barona, another Chicago Boy, who was then replaced in December of 1978 by yet another, Rolph Luders. Alvardo Bardon was Undersecretary for the Economy in 1982. Chicago Boys also controlled the Central Bank, the Budget Office, and the National Planning Office.

One of the most important Chicago Boys (though he actually went to Harvard for his graduate work, rather than to Chicago) was Jose Pinera. Pinera, the older brother of Sebastian Pinera, was Secretary of Labor and Social Security from 1978 to 1980 and then Secretary of Mining in 1980 and 1981. In the first position, Pinera instituted *three* of the most notable and audacious reforms of the entire tenure of the military government, all of which will be discussed in later chapters. Pinera is also well known for having confronted Pinochet at a cabinet meeting in April of 1981 and talked him out of banishing the radical labor leader Manuel Bustos.

It is true that after Pinera resigned from the Ministry in December of that year, Bustos was in fact exiled. Pinera's action, however, and the fact that he wrote many articles in subsequent years promoting the return of democracy in Chile, must qualify claims by Valdez and others that the Chicago Boys favored continued authoritarian rule in Chile. None of them were opposed to democracy as such. They only opposed unlimited majority rule and the rent seeking and oppression that such majoritarian democracy always generates, and had in fact previously generated in Chile.

NOTES

1. This was attested to by witnesses at the time, including medical doctors at *La Moneda*. It has, of course, become an article of faith among Allende's supporters that he was murdered.

2. Nobody was killed in the raid on the Neltume police station, but the rapidity with which this counterattack had occurred made clear to the Junta the necessity to cut as many heads off the communist hydra as they could, as quickly as possible.

3. Robert L. Scheina, *Latin America's Wars: The Age of the Professional Soldier, 1900 2001* (Washington, DC: Brassey's, 2003), 326.

4. Stern, 53.

5. The Junta members originally planned to have a rotating presidency, but seem to have abandoned that idea and agreed to Pinochet occupying that office permanently. This may have occurred from recognition of his ability and success in that position, or, from a desire for Pinochet, and not them, to be the focus of the inevitable retribution by the left when the Junta eventually left power. One member of the Junta who seems to have resented Pinochet becoming the permanent executive was General Leigh, who was pressured into retirement by the other Junta members in July 1978.

6. The discussion in Stern, 47–53, typifies this interpretation.

7. As cited in William D. Rogers, "Fleeing the Chilean Coup: The Debate over U.S. Complicity," *Foreign Affairs* (January/February 2004).

8. Steven J. Lynton and Lawrence Meyer, "Ex-Chilean Ambassador Killed by Bomb Blast," *The Washington Post* (22 September, 1976).

9. Andrew and Mitrokhin, 87.

10. Valdez, 112-114.

11. Valdez, 117-130.

12. Valdez, 136.

13. William J. Barber, "Chile con Chicago: A Review Essay," *Journal of Economic Literature* 33, no. 4 (December 1995): 1942, following Valdez fairly closely and uncritically, stresses just how uncongenial to Chicago views the intellectual climate in Chile was at the time.

14. Valdez, 209.

15. Valdez, 218.

16. Valdez, 228-229.

17. "Sebastian Pinera," *Wikipedia* (15 August 2010).

18. Valdez, 214-215.

19. Valdez, 201-203.

20. Valdez, 215-217.

21. Valdez, 247-250.

22. Arnold C. Harburger, "Secrets of Success: A Handful of Heroes," *The American Economic Review* 83, no. 2 (May 1993): 343–350, particularly 345–347. Oddly, Harburger does not specifically mention Underagga, who is center stage in Valdez' account of these events.

23. Valdez, 16-18.

24. Edwards and Edwards, 93.

25. Valdez, 17. Valdez' statement here that the Naval elite held classical liberal views is at odds with earlier claims he made to the effect that such views had never had any place in Chilean political discourse before the Chicago Boys introduced them. The Navy had to get them from somewhere.

Chapter Three

The First Phase of Market Reforms

As Allende socialized the Chilean economy, the PDC had moderated because its radical left wing split away and joined the UP. Before the Chicago Boys came to dominate Junta policy making, market oriented reforms began implementation *under guidance of its PDC advisers*. One of the first things they did was to start eliminating the price controls. Since those controls had been deliberately repressing inflation, prices immediately shot up, and the inflation rate that year was over 500 percent.[1] Markets equilibrated, however, ending the shortages. Goods appeared on the shelves once again, the black markets disappeared, and in 1974 the economy began to recover. This quick and obvious success of the policy of freeing the market had a tremendous demonstration effect on the Chilean public, giving them strong reason to support, or at least delay objecting to, further liberalization efforts.

The Junta's next priority was to reduce the inflation by attacking its root causes, but success on this front came more slowly, and with much travail. Several bad policies were intertwined here. One was the massive nationalization of businesses by the Allende government and the enormous increase in government subsidies to such firms, along with the similar expansion of expenditures for income redistribution programs. It was this huge growth of the government sector and decline of the productive private sector that had generated the budget deficit and the monetary expansion to finance it. To the military government and its PDC economic team, it was obvious that their basic program must reverse all of those policies.

The first step was to begin returning the socialized productive assets to the private sector as soon as that could be done in an orderly fashion. There were several reasons for this. For one, the profit and loss incentives of private ownership, guided by market- determined price signals, would allow much more efficient use of the resources and consequently expanded real production and income for Chileans.[2] In addition, the increased growth of real output would in itself be a factor tending to reduce inflationary pressures. The privatized firms would not only stop being a drain on the treasury (since their government subsidies would end), but the increased production and income would expand government tax revenues. Both of those changes would help reduce the budget deficit, and hence the central bank debt monetization that was fueling inflation. For all those reasons, and perhaps others, the Pinochet government began privatizing with dispatch. In 1974 alone it sold off over two hundred of CORFO's firms. By 1978 CORFO only retained control of twenty-three firms (although the government also controlled seventeen other non-CORFO firms). As part of the same effort, the government began privatizing much of the agricultural land that Allende had confiscated for land redistribution and collective farming. For the first time since Allende had taken office, agricultural production in Chile stopped falling and started to rise, as shown earlier in Figure 1.1.

In yet another attack on the structural deficit, the military government replaced the national sales tax with a twenty percent Value Added Tax (VAT) which would raise much more revenue.[3] Similarly, in April of 1975 when Jorge Cauas became Finance Minister in charge of stabilization and appointed Sergio de Castro as Economics Minister they imposed a temporary increase in the income tax rate of ten percent. They also instituted a ten percent consumption tax on luxury items.[4] Here again, the idea was to reduce monetary expansion and inflation by raising tax revenue while reducing expenditures, thus reducing the government budget deficit and debt monetization.

The cumulative effect of these efforts was to reduce the deficit rapidly, in both absolute and relative terms. From 30.5 percent of GDP in 1973 it fell to only 5.4 percent of GDP in 1974. In 1976, the budget actually began a series of annual surpluses that ran through 1981, as shown in Figure 3.1 (note that since the budget balance is measured as tax revenue *minus* expenditures, deficits, in which expenditures exceed revenue, are shown as negative magnitudes, while surpluses are shown as positive magnitudes). Inflation remained stubbornly high, though, falling to 369 percent in 1974, then to 343 percent in 1975, and still being over 84 percent in 1977. Not until the 1980s did the inflation rate fall to Chile's 1960s average of about 24 percent, and it never stabilized below ten percent until the mid 1990s, as Figure 3.2 shows.

Suspecting from the first that their policies might take some time to reduce the inflation rate down to single digit levels, a related goal of the military government was to protect workers from its effects. This may have seemed necessary because *ending* the legal price ceilings initially appeared to make inflation worse, as prices were freed to rise to market clearing levels. Therefore, in October of 1974, the government imposed compulsory wage indexation on employers across the economy, i.e., automatic annual wage

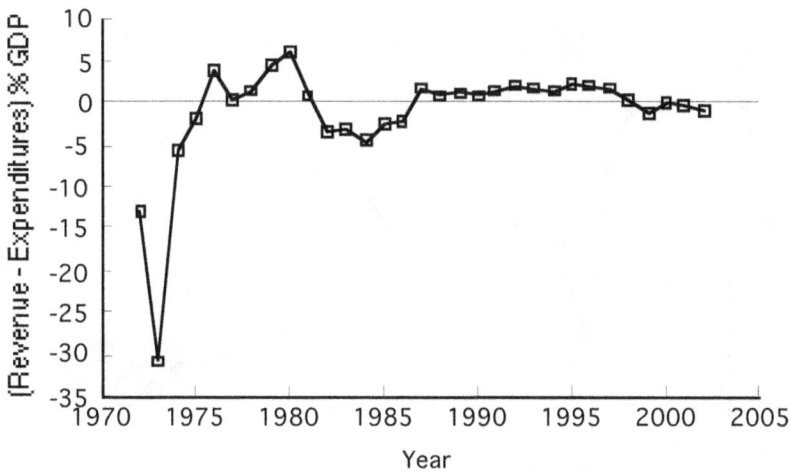

Figure 3.1.   Budget Balance as Percent of GDP. Data Source: Chilean Central Bank.

increases in magnitudes based on official empirical estimates of *prior* inflation rates.[5] The idea—not original, since wage indexation was being advocated by some intellectuals and academics in the United States at the time—
was to prevent the real wage rates of employees, that is, the *purchasing
power* of their earnings, from being reduced as the prices of goods and
services rose.

Not only were wage rates generally subjected to backward-looking indexation, but the general minimum wage was raised in January of 1974 and later
legally required to rise in accordance with the same indexation formula to
prior estimated inflation.[6] The rationale was the same, with the legal minimum simply being targeted at low-skilled, relatively abundant, and hence
low-wage employees. This wage-indexation policy was, unfortunately,
undertaken by the military government either in ignorance of the logical and
the empirical economic effects of such policies, or by deliberately ignoring
them and acting instead to satisfy a powerful set of interests. This caused
severe problems that will be discussed in the next section.

Another fundamental goal of the Junta's first phase of reforms was to free
the foreign sector. Chile badly needed its economy opened to world trade,
ending the long-standing policy of import substitution that had subsidized
and expanded the internal manufacturing sector at the expense of others.
Access to low-cost foreign goods and services would benefit all Chileans,
though there would necessarily be significant pain involved as scarce resources were redistributed internally out of manufacturing and into new export sectors where Chileans would have comparative cost advantages. That

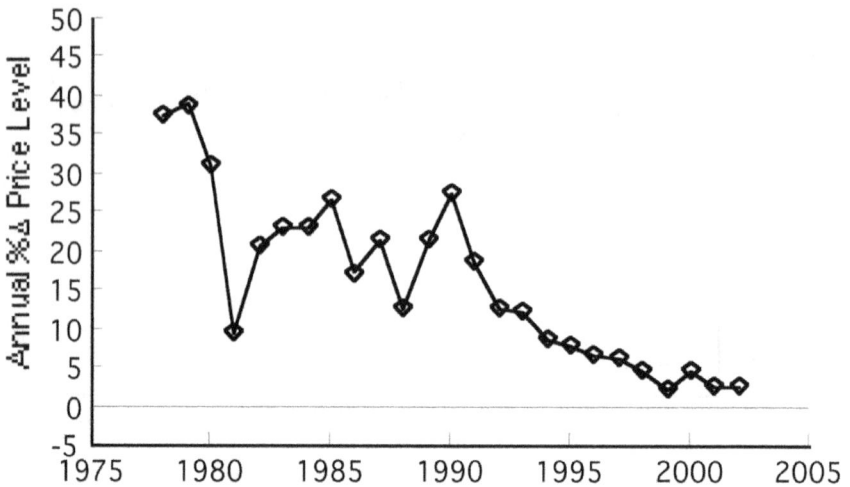

Figure 3.2.   Percent Inflation Rates, 1978-2002. Data Source: Chilean Central Bank.

process would necessarily take time and involve inconvenient dislocations. Equally painful, but just as necessary, was to move toward balance in Chile's external payments and end the trade deficit.

The Junta moved swiftly, starting late in 1973 almost immediately after taking power, and a year and a half before the Chicago boys began being appointed to major policy positions. Government import purchases using foreign exchange reserves of the central bank largely ceased. The complex system of fifteen separate exchange rates for different categories of transactions was simplified to three. The Chilean currency was devalued (the Escudo price per foreign currency raised), while tariffs (taxes) on import goods, which had been averaging over one hundred percent of the value of such goods, were reduced in stages over five years to a uniform ten percent rate. In 1974, interest rates were decontrolled and, like prices of goods and services, they adjusted upward, in this case to add inflation premiums. The government also reduced the fraction of reserves banks were legally required to hold against deposits, and allowed new forms of financial institutions to be formed.

Benefits from the financial reforms—particularly in the banking sector—occurred fairly quickly, but some problems also emerged. The number of financial institutions increased and the real volume of credit (after adjusting for inflation) rose rapidly. Stock market transactions increased, though *initial* stock issues by firms—new capitalization— grew rather slowly. The national saving rate remained low and the liberalization of trade was accompanied by a growing capital account surplus and current account deficit. In essence, Chileans bought and imported a larger volume and value of foreign goods and services than they sold and exported to foreigners. American and other bankers and businessmen then used the Chilean currency thus acquired to make loans and direct investments in Chile. A combination of continuing overvaluation of the Chilean currency (*despite* the large official devaluation in 1973) and high real interest rates in Chile seems to have driven this outcome.[7]

THE CHICAGO BOYS IN CHARGE

Public support for the Pinochet administration's "neoliberal" reform effort at reducing the size and power of the Chilean government and establishing a healthy private sector economy was tested early and suddenly by a very large recession that hit Chile in 1975. Real GDP fell 13.2 percent, as Figure 3.3 shows. Since the intellectual enemies of the military government have tried so hard to blame all of this on its allegedly Chicago inspired "Neoliberal" reforms, it is important to remember two things. First, the Chicago Boys only began to occupy major cabinet positions in April of that year, when the contraction was already underway. Second, the contraction was international in scope, and the events that generated it had their origins outside of Chile.

The initiating factor was the 1973 Mid-East war, which gave the Organ-ization of Petroleum Exporting Countries (the OPEC Cartel) an opportunity and excuse to meet, restrict their collective production (adding to the effect of the war in constricting oil deliveries), and drastically raise the world price of crude oil. This huge cost-push hurt all industrial oil importing nations, including the United States.[8] Chile was also hit hard, however, being over-industrialized *precisely because of its long-standing mercantile import sub-stitution policies,* and unlike some oil-rich Latin nations, it was a net oil importer. True, the contraction was far greater in Chile than in most other industrial nations, but that was due in large part to a steep decline in the world price of copper that year.

Chile was one of the largest national suppliers of that ore on the world market, and copper extraction was a major employer. The decline in the world copper price was itself, in part, an effect of the increase in crude oil prices by OPEC. As the economies of the oil importing nations contracted in 1974 and their manufacturing output and employment declined, their demand for copper to be used in manufacturing and communications fell.[9] This de-layed reaction accounts in part for why the recession was actually delayed in Chile, arriving there a year later than it did in the U.S. and other industrial nations.

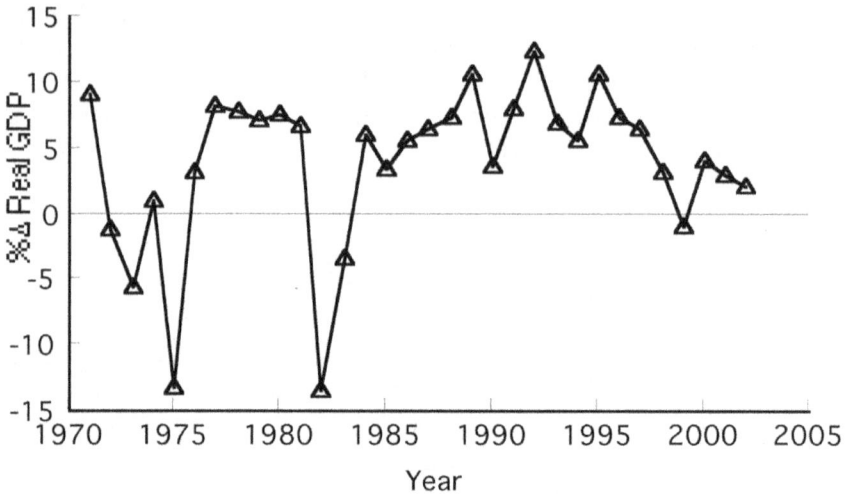

Figure 3.3.   Percent Changes in Real GDP, 1971-2002. Data Source: Chilean Central Bank.

It seems apparent that the actions of the military government in opening the Chilean economy to world trade cannot be assigned much of the blame for the internal impact of the recession. Chile had already over-industrialized itself, was already importing much of its oil for automotive and industrial use, and was already heavily dependent on copper extraction employment and copper export earnings. Those prior conditions would have magnified the contractionary effect of the international recession as it was transmitted to the Chilean economy if there had been no military government and, hence, no free market reform program at all.

This is not to say, however, that *none* of the policy actions of the Junta and its (initially mostly PDC) policy advisers bore any responsibility at all for the magnitude of the 1975 contraction in Chile. The stringent effort to reduce the budget deficit and rate of money stock growth that the Pinochet government was undertaking, given the persistence of high inflation, certainly reduced the purchasing power of money held in Chilean's cash balances, and constrained their purchases, perhaps adding several percentage points to the contraction and raising the unemployment rate accordingly.

Indeed, the Chicago Boys probably bear some responsibility here. When Jorge Cauas became Economics Minister in April, he quickly announced and began carrying out an even more restrictive monetary policy (since known as "The Shock Treatment") than the PDC team had been following. Part of this involved literally replacing the Chilean Escudo in September of that year with a new Peso at a rate of one thousand Escudos per Peso. Unless the PDC advisory team really had already been self-consciously implementing the first steps of *El Laudrillo*, this was the opening salvo in the program of the Chicago boys, which some analysts termed as the *second phase* of the military government reforms. The immediate effect may indeed have added to the contractionary pressures already existing.

Cauas and De Castro must have known that would be the case, at least temporarily. It is possible that they used the recession as cover, knowing that most Chileans were aware of its origin in international oil and copper price shocks, and that it would be difficult for the intellectual and political enemies of the reforms to disentangle the initial contractionary effects of their stringent fiscal and monetary policies from those of the international shocks. Thus, the recession may have been as much of an opportunity as a threat to the program of the Chicago Boys as they began to implement policy. Several things need to be understood here, however. Enemies of the liberation government, some neutral analysts, and even its friends have exaggerated its capacity to do whatever it wanted. Certainly as a military government that was literally purging the populace of its most radical-left elements and that had suspended normal political activity, it could act more freely in its economic reforms than could any democratic government under normal interest group pressures. Still, like every other government from the beginning of human history, it had to satisfy many elements of society in order to retain power, which often meant doing some things that did not exhibit strict economic rationality.[10]

In addition, the capacity of the Chicago Boys to institute anything they desired as they became the regime's dominant policy advisers, has also been exaggerated. Yes, they added depth and clarity over time to the initially hazy large private sector, small-government sentiment the regime started with, but as non-economists in charge, Pinochet and the other Junta authorities often failed to understand, and/or rejected, for personal and political reasons, the advice of the Chicago Boys, and insisted on doing things their own way. Last, the ideological, free market purity of the vision and program of the Chicago Boys has itself been exaggerated. They aimed at replacing the incipient communist system with a strong private sector economy and a moderate regulatory welfare state, but *not* with any *laissez-faire* economic system.[11] If they had, things would have almost certainly gone even better than they did.

Consider the persistence of inflation, despite the strength and stringency of administration budgetary and monetary restriction. That stringency—and the currency reform—should have severely reduced the inflation expectations of the Chilean public and caused inflation to decline more rapidly toward convergence with international inflation rates. Yet, it took nearly a decade to get inflation down to historic Chilean levels, as Figure 3.2 above shows. Why? Also, why did unemployment rates, which doubled from five to ten percent of the labor force in 1974 and rose nearly another five percent-

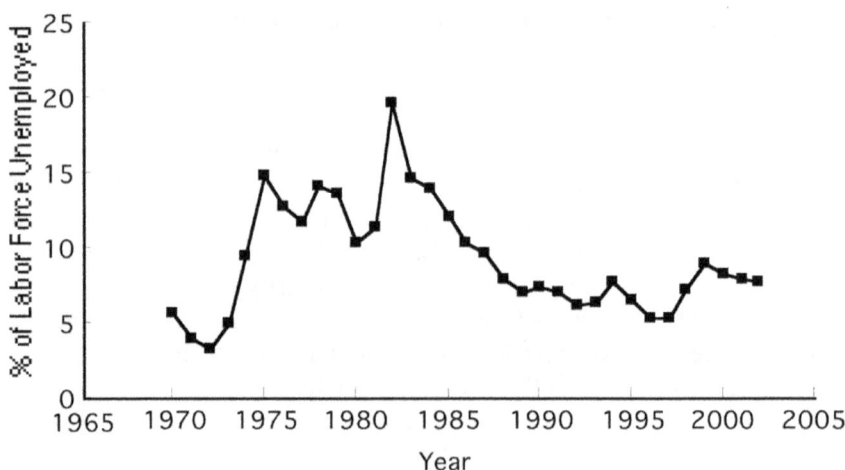

**Figure 3.4.   Percent Unemployment, 1970-2002. Data Source: Chilean Central
Bank.**

age points during the 1975 contraction, stay high for so long afterwards, not
falling into single digit rates until1987?

The primary answer to both questions is that the labor policy of the Junta,
described in the section above, conflicted completely with its budgetary/
monetary efforts. Leftist ideologues ignorant of economics believe every rise
in the real wage is a good thing, but *that is only true when it is a result of
productivity growth.* Just as any legal price floor in a market generates a
surplus of the good or service transacting in that market, real wage rates
forced or kept above the marginal product of labor by extortionate union
action or government diktat generate unemployment, and with it, *reduced*
aggregate production and real income. Success for the Junta's efforts to
reduce inflation and unemployment and raise real income required both price
and wage *inflation* rates to be *flexible,* so they could not only adjust down-
ward, but do so *relative* to one another, reducing the excessive real wage to
its market clearing value. [12]

The administration had freed final product and non-labor service prices
by removing the legal ceilings imposed by Allende, but wage flexibility was
not instituted. In fact, the military government policy of legally indexing
wage rates to *prior* inflation meant that every reduction in the rate of price
increase caused the real wage to rise and squeezed the profitability of employers, thus reducing new hiring, causing layoffs, and putting some firms
out of business. Those pressures both inhibited employers from reducing
their rates of price increases over time and kept unemployment rates high. [13]

The interventionist character of the wage-indexation policy and its total incompatibility with any program of genuine free market liberalization, should be apparent. Equally as apparent should be that the military government was either too confused to see that incompatibility and grasp its harmful effects or was acting to minimize opposition from a powerful segment of Chilean society by placating organized and unorganized employees. Indeed, even as the Chicago Boys began to be appointed to key policy positions in 1975, *they announced that wage indexation tied to prior inflation rates would continue.* It took several years of demonstrated harm from that policy before the government dared to tackle the problem.

Finally, in 1979 the Junta enacted a monumental reform of labor laws designed by Jose Pinera, the Chicago Boy who was at that time Secretary of Labor and Social Security. Union power to fix wage rates at levels so high as to cause disemployment was reduced by making union membership *voluntary*. In addition, thirty days after the start of a strike, union members were legally allowed to bargain *individually*, for themselves. These provisions would allow personal freedom of association for workers and generate increased competition in labor markets.

Yet in a clear concession to the political power of organized labor, even this reform enshrined wage indexation permanently for union members (though it seems to have *removed* such indexation as a requirement for negotiations with *non-union* employees) by requiring firms to offer, in union contract negotiations, at a minimum, a wage *increase* equal to prior price inflation. That provision also applied to the individual negotiations that were allowed after thirty days of an unsettled strike.[14] Worse, Pinera's vital reform did *nothing* to reduce the harm from the excessively high minimum wage— itself a form of compulsory government price fixing—or from its backward indexation.

Similarly the VAT and other tax increases that were implemented in 1975 have little root in any pristine free market, minimal government stabilization program. Market purists would have advocated tax rate *reductions* at that time and circumstance, matched by further government expenditure reductions. If any Chicago Boys suggested this, they must have been overruled. Of course, it could be objected that government expenditures were *already* being rapidly reduced (which was true), both absolutely and relative to GDP. Moreover, the tax increases, though tending to marginally discourage productive activity, were simply replacing an increment of debt finance that was just as harmful in crowding out private investment. Plus, the additional tax revenue would bring balance to the budget more quickly as expenditures declined, thus ending the debt monetization.

That argument is compelling, and its logical failures are very subtle. They all stem from a fixation on the budget and inflation that seems to have afflicted both the initial PDC advisory team and the Chicago Boys. Note first that there is no *necessary* connection between the budget and the level of money growth. With control of the central bank, the Chicago Boys could have simply ceased monetizing debt any time they wanted (assuming the government would let them do so) and used direct monetary control—along with the elimination of wage indexation—to bring inflation down. More importantly, policy advisers fixated on ending the budget deficit, *more than on reducing the size of government*, are likely to think their job done when expenditures fall to equality with revenue, balancing the budget.

Precisely because the *mode* of finance (whether by borrowing or taxation in varying relative degrees and combinations) of a given level of total government expenditure and associated resource extraction from the private sector does *not* matter significantly for real economic activity, but the *magnitude* of expenditure and associated resource extraction from the private sector *does* matter (i.e., above a point necessary to provide vital public services, larger government *hurts* real economic growth) [15] , *raising taxes was a mistake*. It left the size of the Chilean government larger than it should have been, and economic growth smaller than it would have been, had tax rates and revenue been reduced instead, thus necessitating further program and expenditure reductions to reach fiscal balance. [16]

Even the best parts of the reform program sometimes contained mistakes, contradictions, and downsides. For example, it is clear that the method the PDC advisers used to privatize the nationalized business firms was flawed, even though privatization was enormously beneficial to the economy on net. As experience with rapid denationalization of former East Bloc socialist economies since 1989 has shown, it is very difficult to privatize large amounts of productive public assets without those designing and enacting the process succumbing to the temptation to use that power to benefit themselves. [17] This seems to have happened in Chile as well.

Chile's nationalized firms were privatized through sales of their stock shares. Under the rules the regime set, a private citizen could not legally buy more than three percent of a given firm's shares, and other firms and holding companies could not buy more than five percent. Those rules were quickly violated, probably as a result of bribery of various officials, and ownership of the privatized firms became concentrated into large conglomerates that came to be known as *Grupos*. The ten largest *Grupos* controlled 135 of the 250 largest private concerns by 1979 and nearly 70 percent of all corporations traded on the stock exchange. [18]

One might note the inherent contradiction and hypocrisy in the condemnation by socialist critics of this ownership concentration following the sales of previously nationalized productive assets. It is more than a little absurd and disingenuous of them to condemn such concentration in private hands and assert a resulting lack of competition as they do when the prior concentration and lack of competition in the giant communist *Grupo* of the government was so much greater. By that *proper comparison*, the asset sales of the military government not only yielded a huge privatization, but a huge *deconcentration* in ownership of the productive assets.

Nevertheless, things did not work out well for the new private owners of the *Grupos* even though they employed those assets far more efficiently to the public benefit than had the government. Some of the firms being privatized were banks, though most were industrial. Both sectors came under heavy competitive pressure from abroad as the Junta reduced tariffs and devalued the currency, opening up the foreign trade sector. By the late 1970s, more than a few of the firms owned by the *Grupos* were closed down and many others were losing money, though as already mentioned, some others had successfully adjusted to the new competitive environment. Overall it is clear that concentration of productive assets within the *Grupos* was *not* associated with high rates of return on investment. Nevertheless, the complaints by leftist intellectuals about private ownership concentration resulting from the privatization being much greater than it should and could have been were justified. These defects in the privatization policies crafted by the Junta's early (PDC) economic advisers were also well understood by the Chicago Boys, who made corrections when an opportunity arose, as discussed later.[19]

The opening of the foreign trade sector also generated problems, eventually motivating a change in anti-inflation strategy employed by the Chicago Boys. Discouraged by their slow progress in reducing inflation through budgetary control, they decided to attempt to reduce it through foreign exchange manipulation. Over the Junta's first several years, despite their initial currency devaluation, failure to adjust the exchange rate in accord with domestic Chilean and foreign inflation differentials had caused the Peso to become significantly overvalued again. In February of 1978, the government established a "crawling peg" (the *Tablita*) in which the Peso would be devalued in terms of the dollar, at pre-announced intervals and incrementally declining amounts, for up to a year. The crawling peg was conducted until June of 1979, when the declining devaluations were ended and the Chilean currency was simply pegged again at a fixed rate against the U.S. dollar.[20]

The *Tablita* did not work well, as most analysts now admit. The Chilean inflation rate certainly did decline in 1978, to only 37.2 percent from over 87 percent the year before, but then essentially stabilized through 1979, falling very little. Because the devaluations occurred at less than the inflation rate differential with the currencies of other nations, the Chilean currency actually became *increasingly* overvalued. Among other things, this overvaluation of the Peso on international markets made foreign credit inexpensive to Chileans. Consequently, many Chilean firms in *Grupos* borrowed large amounts of money from New York banks. Many of those firms that were not doing well against the foreign competition kept borrowing in hopes of recovering from their losses, and the point at which they would have to default was already rapidly approaching by the late 1970s.

Note here again the lack of philosophic consistency in the Junta's allegedly "Neoliberal" policy. *There is nothing* (classical) *liberal about fixed exchange rates*, nor are they consistent with a program aimed at a free economy, with prices set by suppliers and demanders through voluntary exchange. A foreign exchange rate is just the relative price of two currencies and fixing prices is fixing prices. If the fixing of consumer good prices is understood as harmful, due to the shortages or surpluses thus generated, *fixing exchange rates should be looked at the same way because they have the same effects*— in this case generating international payments imbalances. As for exchange rate manipulation as a technique for reducing inflation, that was not only ineffective, but inconsistent with efforts to reduce unemployment as long as wage rates were indexed to prior inflation.[21] What was really needed was flexible market-determined prices in *both* labor *and* foreign exchange markets.

Milton Friedman, who is understood by all as the greatest of Chicago School economists in the mid twentieth century, and was responsible more than any other for the free-market orientation of that school, had long been an advocate of floating exchange rates.[22] This position, long belittled, was vindicated when Richard Nixon closed the Gold Window at the Federal Reserve and ended the Bretton Woods system of fixed exchange rates in 1971. That stopped the drain of American gold to foreign central banks and simultaneously ended the international balance of payments crisis that had plagued all major nations since the mid 1960s. Certainly the Chicago Boys in Chile were aware of all this. Corbo and Fischer even report that a faction of the Chicago Boys advocated a flexible exchange rate system for Chile but lost out in the policy determination process within the Pinochet government.[23]

Despite such errors, it should be admitted that all criticisms of the Pinochet reform policies, including those just made by the present author, consist of Monday morning quarterbacking, and there is no easier game than that. The people in charge at the time had a much more difficult job. In this regard, it must be stressed that the policy decisions that Pinochet and the Chicago Boys got right on the economy far outweighed their mistakes. The 1975 recession bottomed out quickly and real GDP rose every year for the next six years at an average annual compound rate of 6.8 percent, thus raising Chilean production and real income by over 48 percent.[24] Factoring in population growth, real income *per Chilean* rose nearly 39 percent over those six years.

This rapid economic growth helped bring down the rate of inflation, which finally fell below 10.0 percent in 1981. It also helped reduce the unemployment rate, which, though still high, fell to 10.4 percent and 11.3 percent in 1980 and 1981, respectively. By that time even many of the intellectual, academic, and political enemies of the military government were speaking of a "Chilean economic miracle" and had begun to rethink their economic perspectives. In 1982, however, the next recession hit.

NOTES

1. See Corbo and Hernandez, 120 (Table 5.1). This is a refined estimate. The situation at the time was so chaotic that for years reliable data was not available. Early estimates of the 1973 inflation rate often cited it as in excess of 600 percent.

2. Since Britain and many West European nations nationalized some of their industries over the first three quarters of the 20th century, and often nationalized different ones, it has been easy for economists to compare efficiency of private and publicly owned firms and industries of the same types. They regularly found that those privately owned and operated in the market functioned at much higher efficiency and lower costs than the publicly owned equivalents. See Andrei Shleifer, "State Versus Private Ownership," *The Journal of Economic Perspectives* 12, no. 4 (Fall 1998): 133-150; The World Bank, *Bureaucrats in Business: The Economics and Politics of Government Ownership* (New York: Oxford University Press, 1995), 33-41; and John Hilke, *Cost Savings from Privatization: A Compilation of Study Findings* (Los Angeles, CA: The Reason Foundation, 1993).

3. Corbo and Hernandez, 122.

4. Edwards and Edwards, 29–31.

5. Vittorio Corbo and Stanley Fischer, "Lessons from the Chilean Stabilization and Recovery," in *The Chilean Economy, Policy Lessons and Challenges*, eds. Barry Bosworth, Rudiger Dornbush, and Raul Laban (Washington, DC: The Brookings Institution, 1994), 45.

6. Edwards and Edwards, 150–151.

7. Edwards and Edwards, 54–78.

8. See Neil H. Jacoby, *Multinational Oil* (New York: Macmillan, 1974), 257–267; and Council of Economic Advisers, *The Economic Report of the President* (Washington, DC: US Government Printing Office, 1975), 19, 43, 75, and elsewhere.

9. In subsequent years the innovation of satellite telecommunications and fiber-optic cable substituted for copper use and further reduced demand for copper. Copper prices did not recover until 1987. See the time series on copper prices in Corbo and Fischer, 29-80.

10. Valesco, 403, asserts that the military government had goals besides maximizing community welfare, or at least weighted community groups differently, claiming in illustration that costs of its structural adjustment were imposed much more heavily on labor than on business. It is true, for example, that the military government sometimes used force to overcome union resistance to such policies as divestitures that often meant the laying off of redundant state employees by the private buyers. Ultimately, however, the Junta went too far in efforts to *protect* labor and cater to union sensibilities, to the detriment of the economy itself.

11. To illustrate, though the massive subsidies and income redistribution of the Allende administration were largely removed, government aid was specifically retained for, and targeted to, the poor.

12. See Richard K. Vedder and Lowell E. Gallaway, *Out of Work: Unemployment and Government in Twentieth-Century America* (New York: Holmes & Meier, 1993).

13. Edwards and Edwards, in chapters 4 and 6, elaborate the nature and effects of the military government labor policy in great detail. See also Corbo and Fischer, 37–39, where those authors discuss the problems the wage indexation generated for government efforts to achieve external balance.

14. Since voluntary contract is the very essence of a free society in the classical liberal view, this restriction must have been necessary to make the reform minimally acceptable to the Unions.

15. See, for example, Robert Barro, "Recent Developments in Growth theory and Empirics," *The Journal of Private Enterprise* 14, no. 2 (Spring 1999): 55–91; Gerald Scully, "Unfinished Reform: Taxation and Economic Growth in New Zealand," *The Journal of Private Enterprise* 14, no. 2 (Spring 1999): 92–114; James Gwartney, et al., "The Scope of Govern-

ment and the Wealth of Nations," *The Cato Journal* 18, no. 2 (1998): 163–190; and William Easterly and Sergio T. Rebelo, "Fiscal Policy and Economic Growth: An Empirical Investigation," *Journal of Monetary Economics* 32, no. 3 (1993): 417–458.

16. Scully estimates the optimal government resource extraction from the private sector to be about 20 percent of GDP. However, in 1900, U.S. Federal government expenditure was only 5 percent of GDP, and that was during the longest period of rapid economic growth in US history, ranging from the Civil War to World War I.

17. See Marshall J. Goldman, *The Piratization of Russia: Russian Reform Goes Awry* (New York: Routledge, 2004), and Svetovar Pejovich, "On the Privatization of 'Stolen Goods' in Central and Eastern Europe," *The Independent Review* 10, no. 2 (Fall 2005): 209–229.

18. Edwards and Edwards, 98-101.

19. It is often forgotten by critics of the market reform policies that the Chicago Boys were not yet in power when the privatization policy was first initiated.

20. Edwards and Edwards, 35–40.

21. Most analysts now seem to recognize this. See Corbo and Fischer.

22. See the articles in the section on the Balance of Payments in Milton Friedman, *Dollars and Deficits* (Englewood Cliffs, NJ: Prentice-Hall, 1968).

23. Corbo and Fischer, 46

24. Corbo and Hernandez, 124.

Chapter Four

The 1982 Crisis and Third Phase Reforms

In 1982 and 1983, the Chilean economy was shocked into a contraction that was initially as large as that of 1975, but which lasted longer, thus reaching greater depths. In 1982, real GDP in Chile fell by 13.4 percent, by current estimate of its central bank (Figure 3.3), raising the unemployment rate to just under 20 percent of the labor force (Figure 3.4 in the preceding chapter). The next year real GDP declined by another 3.5 percent, though employment actually increased that year, so that the *unemployment* rate fell back to 14.6 percent. Here again, it is important to understand that the initial contractionary shock originated outside of, and was transmitted to, Chile. In this case, it began in the United States.

The period 1965–1981 is known among economists as "The Great Inflation" in the United States, over which the inflation rate, starting from low levels, rose year by year until it reached, by varying estimates and indices, between 10 and 12 percent.[1] America had experienced far worse periods of inflation in its past: during the Revolutionary War, the Civil War, and both of the world wars in the twentieth century. The inflation of 1965–1981, however, was a peacetime inflation, which by the late 1970s appeared to be getting out of control. It literally fed on itself as citizens adjusted their inflation rate expectations upward, reduced their demands for real cash balances, and tried to spend their dollar balances down.[2]

Though even a 12 percent annual rate of price increase seems paltry in comparison to the inflation problem the Chicago Boys faced in Chile, the U.S. inflation was worrisome to a populace used to much lower rates of price rise. The causes of the U.S. and Chilean periods of inflation were similar. Since at least 1949, economic growth had been rapidly *reducing* both the official poverty rate and the *number* of poor Americans. In 1949 there were approximately 49 million Americans living below the official U.S. poverty line and in 1965 there were only 28.5 million. This was a reduction of over 42 percent *despite significant population growth* over that interval.

In that latter year, 1965, however, President Lyndon Johnson announced a War on Poverty, and two years later, in 1967, the government began a massive expansion of U.S. welfare state spending. That expansion continued under Presidents Nixon, Ford, and Carter, before leveling off. Between 1966 and 1980, income transfer payments went from 6.5 to 12.0 percent of total personal income in the U.S. Over the same period, constant dollar public aid expenditures *per poor person* in the U.S. doubled, and by 1996 they had quadrupled.[3]

Unwilling to face the voters up front with the actual costs of these redistributive expenditures through open, legislated tax increases, the federal government financed most of them instead by running successively larger budget deficits (rising even as a percent of GDP), borrowing the money, and having the Federal Reserve monetize much of the added debt.[4] Worse, as people responded to the altered incentives of the increased payments for being poor, the labor force participation rates of low-income Americans dropped. The U.S. poverty rate quickly *stopped* falling, and then started *rising*. With a rising population, this slow upward drift in the poverty *rate* caused the absolute *number* of poor persons in the U.S. to grow rapidly. From 27.8 million in 1967, it had risen to 29.3 million in 1980, a 5.4 percent

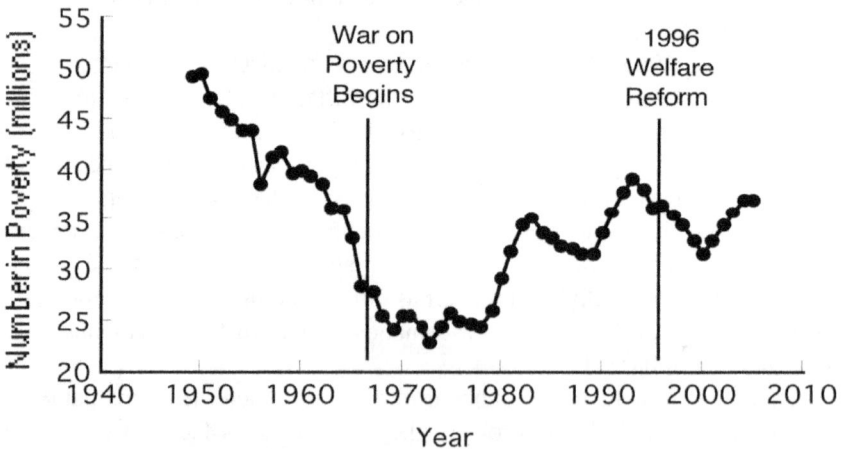

Figure 4.1.   Millions of Poor Americans, 1949-2005. Data Sources: 1949-1958 observations from Bureau of the Census, Current Population Reports. 1959-2006 observations are from The Economic Report of the President, 2008.

rise. By 1996, the year in which the broken system was reformed, it had reached 36.5 million, an increase of 31.3 percent.[5]

By 1979 the political costs to elected federal authorities of this policy of deceptively financing income redistribution and repudiating federal debt through inflation began to exceed its benefits to them, so they ended it.[6] Paul Volker was appointed Chairman of the Federal Reserve Board. He immediately raised the interest rate targets of the Fed and began a contractionary monetary policy aimed at reducing inflation. Within a year or so, debt monetization ceased. With a lag, this policy took hold and generated a large double-dip recession in 1981 and 1983 (with a short, false recovery in 1982). The recession spread internationally—when the U.S. coughs it seems the world catches a cold—and Chile was, again, impacted particularly hard.

As the men in charge in 1981, subject only to the higher authority of the military government, the Chicago Boys cannot escape some of the blame for the enormity of the Chilean contraction of 1982–1983, though simple bad luck also played a part. Fixed exchange rates automatically transmit national macroeconomic shocks internationally, and as the year in which the U.S. began its contractionary monetary policy, 1979 was a particularly bad year for the Chicago Boys to peg the Chilean Peso to the dollar. The rise in real U.S. interest rates after 1979 pushed Chile's foreign debt burden to the limits of their capacity to finance interest and principal payments through earnings, or refinance through additional borrowing. Then, the contraction in American demand for foreign—including Chilean—imports, as the U.S. economy fell into recession in 1981, reduced Chilean export earnings. That further diminished the capacity of Chilean firms to pay their American and Chilean creditors. Output and employment fell massively. Some firms, including several major banks in Grupos and even the whole CRAV Grupo itself, went under, and many other firms teetered on the brink of collapse.

For a while the Chicago reform advisers resisted taking action, openly arguing that the bankruptcies would ultimately be beneficial and that the market should be allowed to adjust by itself. This made the public furious with the military government and its Chicago advisers, however, and there were violent protests in the streets. Bowing somewhat to public pressure, the government shuffled its economic team, replacing some Chicago Boys with others, and began taking action in January of 1983. Two banks were liquidated and some of the firms in trouble—including nineteen financial institutions— were temporarily renationalized. The Chilean Central Bank assumed their foreign debt, trading government bonds for non-performing loans.[7] In addition, tariffs were temporarily raised to provide competitive relief to manufacturers and other exporters and the currency was devalued by 18 percent.

These policy actions represented a significant setback to the liberation government's policy of establishing a stable, self-regulating market system with a small government. Leftist critics of the market reforms felt vindicated.

The set-back was only temporary, however. Within a few years, the tariffs were brought back down and the renationalized corporate firms were privatized again, *this time by a process carefully monitored to insure widespread ownership* and avoid anything like the former *Grupo* concentration.[8]

In addition, the Chicago Boys quickly began the third phase of liberalizing reforms. First, and most important, general wage indexation was finally abandoned in June of 1982.[9] Also, apparently realizing that their earlier tax policy had been a mistake, a new tax law was enacted in 1984 reducing the corporate income tax rate and providing encouragement to saving and investment by allowing reinvested profits to be tax free. Double taxation of corporate investors was eliminated by allowing Chilean stockholders a tax credit usable on their personal income taxes equal to their proportional share of the corporate income tax paid by the company.[10]

One of the biggest problems the Chicago Boys faced was how to deal with the foreign debt burden that Chilean firms had built up, which was a huge impediment to recovery. It should be remembered that Chile in the 1980s was *not* alone in this problem. Firms in *many* Latin American and other Third World nations at the time had borrowed large amounts from American and other developed country banks. Those firms were to the point of default and were looking for ways out. Of course their preferred solution was debt forgiveness, while the New York and other Western banks wanted repayment. As a compromise, rescheduling of debts, a form of partial default and partial repayment, were negotiated in many cases.

Some Monetarist (Chicago School) economists in the U.S. offered an innovative solution, however, pointing out that Third World firms could *always* pay their debts, no matter how great the burden, as long as they had physical assets. All they had to do was trade equity (stock shares) in the indebted firms to their foreign creditors in exchange for their debt.[11] Few Third World nations found this solution palatable, however, and the idea was heavily criticized by economists and academics of the left everywhere as being inherently exploitative and unworkable.

In Chile, however, Pinochet took the advice of the Chicago Boys, and such debt-equity swaps became the preferred solution. As a policy, it worked extremely well, contrary to the predictions of the critics. In 1982, Chile had a foreign debt burden equivalent to $17.4 billion in U.S. dollars, one of the highest per-capita in the world. Yet in only four years, 1985—1989, $10.5 billion of this debt was retired, mostly through various forms of debt-equity swap, and the country had built up $9 billion in foreign exchange reserves. Exports expanded and the country prospered.

RESULTS AND CRITIQUES OF THE MARKET REFORMS

Even in this third phase of reforms several statist inconsistencies were included, such as a new antitrust law and specification of legal rules designed to prevent monopoly price setting by publicly owned 'natural' monopolies such as electrical utilities. The utilities should have instead simply been privatized, with open entry legally established. [12] Nevertheless, the liberalizing reform elements dominated, and the results were astounding. The economy began to recover quickly after reaching bottom in 1983. Indeed, productivity growth raised real GDP at an average compound rate of 6.2 percent per year through the remaining tenure of the military government ending in 1990, as Figure 3.4 in the preceding chapter shows. That growth raised the real income of Chileans over 52 percent and by nearly 40 percent per capita. Opposition to market liberalization dissipated again, even among most of the hard-core elements of the Chilean intellectual and academic left.

Remaining intellectual and academic critics of the liberation government attempt to disparage its economic achievements by attributing the *entire* magnitude of the contractions of 1975 and 1982- 1983 to the "Neoliberal" market reform policies of the Chicago Boys. It is as if there were no external factors at all, and as if decades of income redistribution and import substitution policies bore no responsibility. They also seem to ignore one other crucial fact. The 1980s have been termed a 'lost decade' for Latin American nations, since *almost none of them experienced positive growth in real income per-capita over that whole time, and in most of them it actually declined.* Chile stands out both as the Latin nation that liberalized the most and as the one that actually prospered. [13]

When faced with such undeniable facts about the growth of average gross and per-capita real income generated in a market economy, of course, men of the left always have one other resort: complaint about its distribution. They claim that all of the gains go to the rich and the poor may even be worse off. Steve Stern, for example, asserts that economic inequality in Chile had widened in this period. Specifically, Stern says the income share of families in the bottom two quintiles (40 percent of all families), already only 14.1 percent in 1978, had fallen further to a mere 11.8 percent by 1988. Meanwhile, the income share of people in the top quintile, at 51.9 percent in 1978, had risen further to 60.4 percent in 1988. [14]

Several points are in order. First, without denying that a widening of the Chilean income distribution occurred, it does not follow, as many people might assume, that such a widening of the gap between rich and poor need be associated with a decline in *absolute* income of people in *any* quintile. In the U.S. during the very same period, the income share of the top quintile rose while that of the bottom quintile fell, just as it did in Chile. Yet it turned out that the mean real (inflation adjusted) income of people in *all five* quintiles *rose*. It simply increased more for the upper quintile. Given the rapid rise in mean real income in Chile from 1975–1981 and then after the 1982–1983 recession, this might well have happened there also.

Second, those who chronically complain about the income distribution in free market economies—as Chile was rapidly becoming—never seem to take into account vertical economic mobility, which may be enormous. When the U.S. Treasury department tracked the members of 14,351 American families for the decade from 1979 to 1988, they found that in each year about 18 percent of those who began the year in the lowest quintile moved *up* one or more quintiles, while about 20.0 percent of those who began the year in the top quintile moved *down* one or more by the year's end. Over the whole decade, only 14.2 percent of those who began in the *lowest* quintile in 1979 were still there in 1988, while 14.7 percent of those who began in the lowest quintile had made it clear into the *top* quintile. In short, for those who began poor, the probability that they would still be poor a decade later was actually *smaller* than the probability that they would end the decade among the *wealthy*.[15]

When the Institute for Social Research at the University of Michigan conducted a similar study tracking the persons in a huge sample of families from 1975 to 1991, they found that the average income gain over that period by those who started in the bottom quintile was $25,322 in 1993 dollars. By contrast, the average gain in real income over the period by those starting in the *top* quintile was only $3,974 in 1993 dollars.[16] In short, *following actual persons*, it turned out that the *poor got richer by far more than the rich got richer*, the exact opposite of the impression given by the widening income quintile differential during the period!

The rise in inequality between the top and bottom quintile shares in the United States seems to have been mostly a result of those moving up from lower quintiles into the top quintile making large real income gains in the process and displacing in the rankings people who were previously there. It was, in other words, a story of economic success expressed in increased vertical income mobility among the population. This may also have been true of Chileans in that period. Indeed, studies have shown that though income inequality is large in Chile, so is vertical income mobility.[17]

In a market economy, the typical experience is that people leave home or otherwise enter the labor markets as young adults and do not initially earn much because they have comparatively little education, knowledge, experience, or skills. Hence, they fall low in the quintile distribution. Over time, however, by trying different employments they find an occupational niche, gain experience, on-the-job training, and often formal education, all of which enhances their productivity and value in the market, so that they rise through the income quintiles. They also typically get married and have children. Then at the end of their careers they retire and their income drops somewhat. This is called the life cycle of income.

The studies of vertical income mobility in the U.S. referenced above all show that families average smaller and younger in the lower family income quintiles and larger and older in the upper quintiles. Fifth (top) quintile families have an average of three times as many employed members as those in the lowest (first) quintile, which accounts by itself for no small part of the difference. Thus, with qualifications for those few who become super-rich and those few who through bad fortune or lack of ambition remain chronically poor through their lives, *much of the difference in income between people in the different quintiles is simply a matter of what stage they are in at that point in time in their life cycle.*

In that regard, economist Don Mathews demonstrated some years back how little useful information is actually conveyed by the quintile income distribution by itself. He constructed an imaginary economy in which every person began work at age 21, obtained a 6 percent raise at the end of each year, and retired at age 65. Thus the *lifetime* incomes of all citizens were *identical*, though at every point in time each annual population cohort was at a different stage in life. Yet, the quintile income distribution obtained in any year was a 5.4 percent share of aggregate income for the 1st quintile, 9.1 percent for the second, 15.4 for the third, 26.0 for the fourth, and 44.0 for the top quintile, which was amazingly similar to the actual U.S. quintile distribution.[18] From this and what was said above, it should be clear that the quintile income distribution alone is not just *uninformative* about existing equality/inequality and what is happening in the lives of the real persons in society, but highly *misinformative*.

NOTES

1. *The Economic Report of the President* (Washington, DC: US Government Printing Office, 2010), Table B-3 (286) shows GDP Deflator inflation rate values of 9.1 percent for 1980 and 9.4 percent for 1981. Table B-63 (357) shows CPI inflation rate values of 12.5 percent for 1980 and 8.9 percent for 1981. The GDP deflator values are probably by far the more accurate of the two estimates.

2. These estimates are from data in Bureau of the Census, *Current Population Reports*, and from the Council of Economic Advisers, The *Economic Report of the President* (Washington, DC: US Government Printing Office, 1988), Table B-30, and the same source, 2004, Table B-33.

3. Calculated by the author from data in U.S. Department of Commerce, *Statistical Abstract of the United States* (Washington, DC: U.S. Government Printing Office, various years), section on Social Insurance and Human Services, adjusted by GDP Deflator values and the number of poor persons taken from *The Economic Report of the President*, 2004, Tables B-3 (288), and B-33 (324).

4. The incentives that congress, various presidents, and the monetary authorities acted upon in this episode are examined in James Rolph Edwards, "The Financial Pathology of The Postwar American Welfare State," *New Perspectives on Political Economy* 5, no. 2 (2009): 81–109. Daniel Thornton demonstrated that the Federal Reserve monetized much of the federal

debt incurred during the period of the "Great Inflation." See Thornton, "Monetizing the Debt," Federal Reserve Bank of St. Louis Review 66 (December 1985): 30–43.

5. *The Economic Report of the President*, 1988, Table B-30 (282), and 2004, Table B-33 (324). Percent change calculations by author.

6. James Rolph Edwards, "The Financial Pathology of the Postwar American Welfare State," 99–105.

7. Over time, the central bank suffered huge losses on that debt, equaling 7.8 percent of GDP in 1985 alone.

8. Corbo and Hernandez, 130–131; Gallego and Loayza, "The Golden Period of Growth in Chile: Explanations and Forecasts," in *Economic Growth: Sources, Trends, and Cycles*, eds. Norman Loayza and Raimondo Soto (Santiago: Central Bank of Chile, 2002), 417–463, comparing performance in the Chilean economy before and after 1985, find that the sectors subject to privatization did particularly well.

9. Corbo and Fisher, 39.

10. Corbo and Hernandez, 130.

11. Perhaps the first aggressive advocate of debt-equity swaps to solve third-world indebtedness problems was the Monetarist economist Alan H. Meltzer, "Five Reasons for Opposing the IMF Quota Increase," in *Constructive Approaches to the Foreign Debt Dilemma* (Taxpayers' Foundation: 1983), 9–11. Meltzer, however, credits the idea to Wilson Schmidt, President Reagan's nominee to be the American Executive Director to the World Bank, some years later.

12. In the year 2000, when the state of Michigan passed Public Act 141 removing the section from its regulatory law legally *forbidding* entry, new private firms entered the market *almost immediately* and electricity prices fell. See Theodore Bolema, "Re- regulating Electricity Could Shock Michigan's Economy," Mackinac Center for Public Policy *Viewpoint on Public Issues* (16 August, 2004). Rate regulation and entry prohibitions, common to all states, had certainly not been protecting Michigan consumers from monopoly pricing, but *protecting a legally franchised monopoly* (two, actually, in separate geographic regions of the state) *from competition*, at the *expense* of the public. The electrical franchises and rate regulation that states adopted in the early 20th century was almost certainly a simple result of successful rent-seeking, not of natural monopoly. See Greg A. Jarrell, "The Demand for State Regulation of the Electric Utility Industry," *Journal of Law and Economics* 21 (October 1978): 269–295, and George Stigler and Clair Friedland, "What Can Regulators Regulate? The Case of Electricity," *Journal of Law and Economics* 6 (October 1963): 1–16.

13. See Gallego and Loayza, 421. That this differential experience was due precisely to the liberalizing policies undertaken by the Chicago Boys and not taken (or taken too late) in other Latin nations is also affirmed by Raphael Bergoeing, Patrick J. Kehoe, Timothy J. Kehoe, and Raimundo Soto, "Policy-Driven Productivity in Chile and Mexico in the 1980s and the 1990's," *The American Economic Review Papers and Proceedings* 92, no. 2 (May 2002): 16–21.

14. Stern, 350.

15. U.S. Department of the Treasury, Office of Tax Analysis, *Household Income During the 1980s: A Statistical Assessment Based on Tax Return Data* (June 1, 1992). See also Elizabeth V. Sawhill and Mark Condon, "Is U.S. Income Inequality Really Growing?" *Urban Institute Policy Bites* no. 13 (Washington, DC: June 1992).

16. As cited by W. Michael Cox and Richard Alm, "By Our Own Bootstraps: Economic Opportunity and the Dynamics of Income Distribution," Federal Reserve Bank of Dallas, *Annual Report* (1995).

17. Florencia Torche, "Unequal But Fluid: Social Mobility in Chile in Comparative Perspective," *American Sociological Review* 70, no. 3 (June 2005).

18. Don Mathews, "Does an Unequal Distribution of Income Justify Government Redistribution?" *Journal of Private Enterprise* 14, no. 1 (Fall 1998): 68–85, particularly 69–70.

Chapter Five

Social Security Reform

Three of the most important and innovative market oriented reforms under-taken by the liberation government late in its *second phase* of reforms have not yet been mentioned because they deserve special and separate discussion. Two of these historic, daring, and imaginative reforms were designed and guided through the policy making process by Jose Pinera. The first of these was a reform of Chile's social security system passed into law in 1981, and the second was an educational reform program established that same year.

In the late 1970s, demographic changes similar to those now occurring in the United States—an aging of the population expanding the fraction of the public drawing retirement payments and diminishing the fraction paying into the system—were pushing Chile's retirement system toward bankruptcy. When it began in the 1920s, there were twelve current workers paying into the system per retiree collecting benefits. By 1979, however, it was down to 2.5 current contributors per retiree. Though originally the Chilean pension system was partly capitalized by investing excess revenue collections over current payout in financial markets, it had devolved into a Pay-As-You-Go (PAYGO) system much like that in the U.S. and in most European nations. Benefits escalated quickly to the point that the system had to be subsidized from other tax sources, and the system devolved into a morass of over 100 different retirement regimes greatly favoring upper and middle class work-ers.[1]

Aside from being compulsory, dishonest in their claims, and subject to the demographic problem just discussed, PAYGO systems have other objec-tionable characteristics and affects.[2] Perhaps most important, by convincing people that they need not take much in the way of personal action to secure their retirement because "the government has taken care of it," these defined-benefit systems reduce people's incentives to save. That reduces the aggregate saving rate, diminishing the flow of savings into the financial capital pool, hence reducing physical capital investment, and with it, the growth of productivity, production, and real income.[3]

PAYGO systems are essentially government-run Ponzi schemes, as their early proponents were both well aware and proud of.[4] The central feature of a Ponzi scheme is that *nothing productive is done with the money paid into the system.* Early investors are paid interest on their investments from the contributions of later investors. Private Ponzi schemes are recognized as inherently fraudulent and are illegal. Yet, PAYGO compulsory government retirement systems have the same features. The contributions of current employees, in the form of dedicated taxes, are simply redistributed between generations, from the young to the old. Also, like all Ponzi schemes paying early investors off with the contributions of later investors, they eventually collapse.

The contrast with private retirement systems is stark. Those systems take *voluntarily contracted* contributions of current employees and invest them in the financial markets. That *adds* to the financial capital pool available for investment in productive physical assets and literally generates both the future income to finance the future retirement payments and the future output available for consumption upon retirement. When retirement pensions are fully funded in this manner, it does not matter if a given population cohort is large or small since each cohort generates the future income and output to provide for their own retirement.[5]

To deal with the impending crisis in Chile, Jose Pinera and other Chicago Boys talked the liberation government into instituting a radical free-market reform. The Chilean social security accounts would be privatized with each employee's retirement tax payments becoming his/her personal property. The worker would choose from a government specified set of private competing companies (known as AFPs) one that would invest and manage the funds, and was also allowed to decide, within wide limits, how much to contribute, though the legal minimum was 10 percent of his or her earnings. At retirement at age 65, the accumulated earnings (principle plus interest minus administrative costs) would either be converted into an annuity or paid out as a set of lump sums at the worker's discretion.

To provide a hedge against severe downturn in the market, a minimum pension was guaranteed. Workers could also choose to remain in the old system if they wished, but as the new system was established, ninety percent joined. Of course, diverting the payments of current workers joining the new privatized system away from payments to current retirees meant that the payments to current retirees under the old PAYGO system had to be financed some other way. Under the new law, the liberation government essentially committed the nation to running an annual fiscal surplus for as long as required to fund these "transition costs."[6]

The new privatized system caused a huge rise in the Chilean savings rate to 25 percent of income. By providing such large financial resources to capital markets and hence raising physical capital stock growth, the system of private retirement accounts is properly credited with making a large contribution to the rapid growth in Chilean production that began at the end of the 1982 recession and continued through the remainder of the twentieth century. That growth not only greatly raised real gross and per-capita incomes of Chileans, but the pension earnings of individual retirees increased between 51 and 57 percent in real terms even though their retirement taxes were reduced from 50 percent to only 20 percent of after tax earnings.[7]

Chile's pension privatization had an enormous demonstration effect, though perhaps not as large as it should have had. America and European nations are virtually all facing the same crisis that Chile did as their population ages. At least twenty-eight nations worldwide have partly followed the Chilean example of moving toward a fully funded system, but none have gone as far as Pinochet and the Chicago Boys did, hence none have experienced the same degree of benefits. George H. W. Bush made a halfhearted attempt to follow the Chilean example, suggesting that a mere two percentage points of U.S. worker's contributions be invested in private accounts, but the suggestion went nowhere in the *Republican* Congress. The U.S. social security system, previously forecast to go into the red and having to raise taxes to maintain funding of the PAYGO system sometime around 2016 as the post World War II baby boom cohorts retired, actually found itself with revenue insufficient to cover outlays in 2010. Apparently the forecasters failed to adequately account for the effects of U.S. economic cyclicity.

EDUCATION REFORM

The changes in the Chilean educational system legislated in 1981 were just as radical a free-market reform as was the overhaul of the retirement system. Under Allende, all primary and secondary schools had been taken over and operated by the central government. Enrollment in primary schools was already high by the late 1970s, at around 95 percent, but a much smaller fraction of appropriate age Chileans were enrolled in the secondary schools. Among Latin American nations, Chileans did not rank particularly high in either language or math achievement.

Public education systems, in their nature, have several bad features. First is the compulsory character of both their tax finance and attendance requirements. Second, as socialized institutions, they tend to become heavily bureaucratized and operate inefficiently. Third, as tax subsidized institutions facing parents with zero marginal cost of their children's attendance, they price out private competition for a large majority of families. That means that the schools are under little market pressure either to perform well in terms of providing a meaningful quality of education, or to keep costs down. [8] Parents lack competitive options, and only children in wealthy families can escape. Worst of all, government operated primary and secondary schools forcibly subject everyone's children, decade after decade, to indoctrination in the social and political views of government employees. [9]

Pinera's reform law, passed by the military authorities, transferred ownership and operation of the public schools back to local government and allowed them to contract out many subsidiary services on a competitive bid basis. That would help the schools control costs. The really radical element of the Chilean reform, however, was to allow students to escape public education altogether by allowing parents to take their allotted share of education tax dollars and use it to enroll their children instead in private schools, if they wished.

Pinera and the other Chicago Boys got this idea from Milton Friedman, who had long argued for modifying public education through a system of voucher funding. A voucher is simply a check for their share of education funds that parents of a family may spend where they wish, on the public or *private* school of their choice. The basic idea is to raise pressures on schools to perform better by providing parents with competitive options: the opportunity to switch from a supplier that does not provide a good product (in this case, education of their children) to another that does, just as they have in private product markets. Competition disciplines suppliers, forcing them to provide quality products at competitive prices. Schools, public or private, performing poorly and failing to satisfy parents, will lose customers and revenue. [10]

How has this worked out in Chile? From a classical liberal perspective, the Chilean reform may be criticized for one major divergence from Friedman's pure vision. Herbert Wahlberg reports that public schools in Chile losing many students to private schools are *not* closed, as they should be. Instead, they receive subsidies from municipal governments to make up their funding losses so that their teacher's salaries may still be paid. [11] Clearly, that reduces the competitive pressure on public schools to provide quality education so that losses of students and funding are prevented. Nevertheless, significant competitive pressure does seem to have been provided.

Some Chilean critics have argued that the system is a failure because data shows only a small quality advantage of secular private schools over public schools since the reform, although students enrolled in Catholic schools performed better. [12] That, however, would be precisely the result *expected* from competitive pressures intended to improve the quality of the *public* schools *also*. The competition seems to have had the predicted effect on educational quality overall in Chile. In 2006, Chilean students were top among all Latin nations in their language scores and were second only to Uruguayan students in math scores. [13]

Two other accomplishments of the system are unambiguous. One is that the voucher system attracted many poor and rural students int secondary education, raising enrollment in those schools from only 65 percent of those eligible in 1982 to 90 percent in 2003. That affect alone greatly increased the education level of Chileans overall. The most important accomplishment of the voucher system, however, is that, as of 2002, *almost one-half* of Chilean students were attending private schools. [14] The monopoly capacity of the Chilean political and intellectual left to indoctrinate *everyone's* children at the primary and secondary level in *their* views generation after generation has ended.

The Chilean voucher system has not had the demonstration effect on the rest of the world that the pension reform had. For one thing, at least one nation, the Netherlands, had instituted vouchers on a large scale long before the Chilean reform. Originating in 1917, the Dutch system provides vouchers for students wishing to attend religious and private not-for-profit schools, which now enroll 76 percent of all primary and secondary students. More-over, the Dutch are not the only country employing vouchers on a wide scale. In 1993, Sweden passed a law providing funding equal to 85 percent of per-pupil *public* school funding for use in *private* schools chosen by parents, including for-profit schools. Walberg cites studies reporting that this in-creased competitiveness both raised student achievement and improved pa-rental satisfaction with their children's schools. [15]

Among the United States, both Vermont and Maine have had functioning voucher systems in some of their districts for a long time. [16] Yet in the public debate over vouchers during the administration of George H. W. Bush, virtu-ally all of this historical experience, including that of the Netherlands, Swe-den, Vermont, Maine, and the Chilean reform, was ignored despite its rele-vance. Outside of Vermont and Maine, only a few small-scale state level voucher programs are being tried in the U.S. in the face of bitter opposition from teacher unions. A bill establishing a *universal* voucher system actually passed the Utah legislature by one vote and was signed by the Governor in 2009. The teacher unions and school administrators quickly organized and lobbied heavily, outspending voucher proponents to successfully get the law repealed by initiative petition.

In 1991, Colombia, perhaps influenced by the Chilean experience, con-ducted a randomized experiment in which it awarded vouchers covering only part of the cost of education to 125,000 students, chosen by lottery, to be spent in private schools. At the end of the experiment, the winning lottery students had, on average, completed more years of education and scored higher on tests in comparison to lottery losers. [17] Soon more evidence on the effects of competitive education will be available. In 2009, India passed what was called the RTE (Right to Education) Bill, which amounts to the world's largest voucher program for primary education. Despite limits targeting it toward disadvantaged students, provisions for political control of voucher fund use (restricting parental choice), and other problems, within a dozen years about 34 *million* students in India could be attending private schools.

WATER LAW REFORM

Legalized private ownership, not only of consumer goods but also of productive capital assets (equipment, structures, vehicles, etc.) and land, is one of the defining institutional features of modern free societies. Indeed, along with developments in moral and legal systems, language, writing, and technology, the extension of property rights has been a key feature in the emergence of civilization itself. The key cultural transformation that occurred as certain hunter-gatherer tribes first (then others later) became pastoral societies was not just the discovery that certain herd animals could be domesticated, but the idea of *owning*, *breeding*, and *raising* them. Establishing this practice ended the natural tendency toward depletion of such animals from competitive hunting in the wild. Both the persons and the animals involved benefited.

The next cultural transformation, from nomadic pastoral life to settled agriculture, likewise involved not only the discovery of how plants reproduced, but having the idea and adopting the practice of making both the crucial food plants and the land on which they would be grown into *property*. This ended the natural tendency toward depletion of such *plants* from competitive *gathering* in the wild, as the new owners started sowing, watering, fertilizing, harvesting, and resowing the crops. Nomadic life finally ended, since some crops could also augment forage in the feeding of farm animals, though ranchers must still shift their herds among pastures to avoid forage depletion. [18]

The most recent cultural transformation from primarily agricultural economies to modern high-income and long life expectancy industrial societies also began with a transformation of property rights. The medieval system of aristocratic land tenure with semi-communal agriculture was replaced with private farming for the market, as the great landed estates were literally broken up by the British Parliament and deeded out to former serfs as private farms. Owners gained the freedom to buy and sell land, make their own production method and crop type decisions, and then sell their output in free markets for profit. Farmers who were more efficient and profitable bought land and gained market share while those less efficient sold their land and left the market. Agricultural production rose and farmers could feed both themselves and others better. The fraction of the population employed in agriculture thus declined, releasing human resources for non-agricultural employment. [19]

Private ownership of productive capital assets, inventions (patents), and trademarks also became recognized and protected by the law. This aided the incipient industrial revolution that was rapidly drawing employment from the agricultural sector (and nearly emptying the medieval work-houses, poor-houses, and prisons in Britain). Mercantile institutions of state granted monopolies and cartels steadily fell away and true market economies emerged, in Britain, in the U.S.A., then in other settler colonies and in Western Europe. [20] All this occurred as the classical liberal vision of a free society based on private ownership and mutually voluntary interactions between and among *equals*, with allocation of scarce resources to be guided by market price, profit and loss signals and motivated by self-interest incentives, gained greater acceptance.

To this day, however, one of the most scarce and valuable substances on earth, fresh *water*, has seldom had private property rights established so that market exchanges between suppliers (say, for example, canal developers or farmers owning rights) and demanders (other farmers, industrial users, or urban consumers) could generate the price signals and profit/loss incentives allowing and motivating people to economize on its use. Instead, even in the modern market-industrial nations, though some private development and exploitation of water resources has always been allowed, water has generally come to be governmentally developed, managed, and disseminated.

The guiding assumption of the water authorities thus legally established seems to have been that water was an abundant collective asset that should be made available at low or no cost to the users beyond the general taxes necessary to fund the projects (dams, canals, municipal water wells, and sanitation systems, etc.) thought necessary or politically desirable. Consequently, water use, whether agricultural, urban or industrial, is nearly everywhere *subsidized* and underpriced to its users. Predictably, water is almost everywhere *overused*, to the extent of depletion of many sources of supply, including groundwater table reductions in some places, declines in stream flows in others, and so on. [21]

As incomes have risen and Western medical technology has spread in the developing nations, their populations have grown, thus increasing the demand for water. After some point, only higher marginal cost sources can be made available, such as bringing water from greater distances for growing municipalities as consumption exceeds the capacity of nearer sources. Future shortages and rationing seem likely if water does not become fully priced. Urban users paying prices closer to the actual scarcity value for water would take shorter showers, water lawns less, wash cars less frequently, and so on, conserving water use and tending to equate the amounts demanded with the amounts made available.

Economists and water authorities have come to recognize the looming necessity of higher water prices, both in developed and developing nations. So far, however, users benefiting from the subsidies, both urban and rural, have generally been able, through applied political pressure, to resist the necessary increases. One way to solve many of these problems would be to establish a system of secure, legally protected, private property rights to water use. Terry Anderson has suggested doing so on the Prior Appropriation system of "first in time, first in right" (first users have priority in use) applied by some state governments in the American west. [22]

If owners were then allowed to engage in market transactions, farmers having more water use rights than they need could benefit financially by selling to other farmers needing more, and particularly by selling to munici-palities, where water scarcity is most pressing. In principle, absent transac-tions costs, such a market would not only result in water conservation by both urban and rural users, saving much water, but would shift water from lower to higher valued locations and uses until an efficient allocation was achieved, where its value for marginal increments was the same in all uses. Looming water shortages have in fact motivated water authorities to move in the direction of establishing private water use rights and water markets in California, parts of Texas, and other American States.

Some analysts have objected to the creation of water markets on the basis that high transactions costs would prevent trades. It is true that there are significant transactions costs to water rights trades. Costs of search to find a trading partner are an obvious example. These might be low for many local water-use right sales, but higher for interregional trades. Market institutions often arise to reduce search costs, however. Simple want-ad advertising works for many products, for example, and could for water. Either market or governmental institutions for registering water-use rights and transfers would also reduce search costs. Another, perhaps less avoidable transaction cost, is the bargaining to settle terms of contract, and, of course, courts to enforce them.

No doubt, water market trades would involve high costs of literally get-ting the water from its current user to the purchasing user or users in another location. Other transaction costs could be generated by public policy aimed at preventing injury to third parties, harm to fish and wildlife, or other ad-verse environmental impacts. However the bottom line point is this: *all* mar-kets, not just water markets, have transactions costs that limit trades and there simply is no justification for presuming that they are so high as to prevent trades in water altogether. Evidence is overwhelmingly contrary. Informal, local markets in agricultural water use exist in the Western U.S., South America, and many parts of South Asia. [23] If allowed, and if water-use rights were established, registered, and protected in the law, trades would occur on a wider scale. They would take place whenever the value of water to different users, even if they were in different locations, exceeded the transaction costs, just as in any other market for any other resource, product, or service.

Chile provides an excellent example of the feasibility of such markets. It actually has a long history of private development of water resources going back to colonial times. In 1969, however, the Frei government of Christian Democratic (PDC) socialism essentially nationalized all water. From that time through the economic disruptions of the subsequent Allende government and even through the first years of budgetary stringency following the military coup, virtually all development of irrigation systems in Chile ceased. This remained so even though, as shown earlier, agricultural production using existing irrigation systems began to rise again as soon as the Pinochet government removed Allende's price controls (Figure 1.1).

In 1981, with the budget under control, the Chicago Boys saw their opportunity not only to reverse the socialist PDC water policy, restoring the traditional Chilean approach, but to put Chile on the cutting edge of free-market policy by establishing a formal system of recognized private water-use rights and allowing open, formal water markets. The National Water Code defused much potential popular objection by assigning first rights to existing, traditional users. Others wanting rights to unclaimed river, canal or ground water, could obtain them by petition to the authorities (the DGA) in the Ministry of Public Works. The law requires specification of the rights by flow volume per unit of time, though according to Hearne, due to random flow variation in streams, the practical definition actually employed is a share of stream flow.[24] Obtaining of use-rights through purchase is then specifically allowed by the water code. Water use rights are not subject to taxation under the law, but land is subject to property taxation of course, and the value of water, if present, is fully incorporated in the market value of land.

Private and semi-private institutions in the form of independent Water User Associations (WUAs) emerged to diminish transactions costs and facilitate trades. WUAs control all private and even some governmentally created irrigation systems. A WUA is owned by its members who pay fees based on its capital and operating costs. These private groups maintain the canal systems, keep records of right holders, and allocate water to the members based on their right shares. The government does maintain some regulatory authority over this largely private water system. The DGA not only grants the rights (upon petition) for unused water, but plans public investments in the water system. It also intervenes in conflicts over water use, though the courts are the ultimate authority in such cases. When a drought occurs the DGA can also impound water, though it must provide compensation to the owners.

How well has this Chilean experiment in water markets worked? Some research has been completed, with favorable results, and more research is in progress. One historical effect is starkly clear: almost immediately after the law was passed in 1981, private net investment in irrigation systems began again and expanded rapidly. Most of this investment came from entrepreneurial farmers intending to grow fruit and vegetable crops for export. When the military government opened Chile to international trade, such crops were found to be highly profitable on the world market.

Recently, a careful and detailed study of the Chilean water markets by Hearne and Easter, focusing on the upper Maipo River and canal system in Chile's central valley, the Elqui and the Limari Valleys in north-central Chile, and the Azapa Valley in the far north, was completed. They found that transaction costs were not excessive, and there was active trading in all of those areas except for the Azapa Valley, though trades were somewhat infrequent also along the Maipo River. The gains from trade estimated by these researchers in the two areas where trade was most active (the Elqui and the Limari Valleys) were significant.[25]

As with the Chilean innovations in education and social security policy, the daring 1981 National Water Code seems to have had a demonstration effect, as other nations have watched to see what has happened. In recent decades, the nation of Peru, bordering Chile on the North, has been suffering increasingly severe water shortages in its coastal cities, particularly in its capital of Lima, and has had to restrict water use to ration the available supplies. Under this pressure, the government of Peru recently decided to follow the Chilean water policy route. A June 2006 law divested the government of its sole responsibility for constructing water projects and allocating the use of water, shifting to private parties the primary responsibility for managing water use. Like the Chilean water code, the Peruvian law provided for the establishment and marketing of water-use rights, deliberately reducing its own water authorities to a supporting regulatory role.[26]

Neither the Chilean nor Peruvian water laws will turn out to be perfect. No institution, program or policy established by the hand of man is perfect. Chile's water law has already been amended legislatively in efforts to make marginal improvements and such 'tweaking' of the law will no doubt continue. Nevertheless, with its 1981 National Water Code, as in so many other remarkable ways, Chile's military government, under the classical liberal philosophic influence and economic guidance of the Chicago Boys, was successfully able to extend the institutional and policy boundaries defining the free society. The power of the compulsory hand of the state in people's lives has been significantly diminished in the process.

NOTES

1. Sebastian Edwards, "The Chilean Pension Reform: A Pioneering Program," 37–39.

2. See James Rolph Edwards, "Economics, Politics, and the Coming Collapse of the Elderly Welfare State," *Journal of Libertarian Studies* 17, no. 1 (Winter 2003): 1–16.

3. See Isaac Ehrlich and Jian-Guo Zhong, "Social Security and the Real Economy: An Inquiry into some Neglected Issues," *The American Economic Review Papers and Proceedings* 88, no. 2 (May 1998): 151– 157, and Congressional Budget Office, *Social Security and Private Saving: A Review of the Empirical Evidence* (Washington, DC: U.S. Government Printing Office, 1988), 30.

4. A damning quote by Nobel Lauriate economist Paul Samuelson proudly touting the Ponzi character of the social security system is included in Brink Lindsey, "Social Insecurity," *Reason* 33, no. 10 (March 2002): 46.

5. Edwards, "Economics, Politics, and the Coming Collapse of the Elderly Welfare State," 10.

6. See Peter Diamond and Salvador Valdez-Prieto, "Social Security Reforms," in Barry Bosworth, et al., *The Chilean Economy, Policy Lessons and Challenges* (Washington, DC: The Brookings Institute, 1994), 257–327.

7. Sergio Baeza and Raul Burger, "Calidad de las Pensiones del Sistema Privado Chileno," in *Quince Años Despues: Una Mirada al Sistema Privado de Pensiones*, eds. S. Baeza and Francisco Margozzini (Santiago, Chile: Centro de Estudios Publicos, 1995), 165–175.

8. See James S. Coleman, et al., *High School Achievement: Public, Catholic, and Private Schools Compared* (New York: Basic Books, 1982), and Shleifer, "State Versus Private Ownership," 144–148.

9. John R. Lott, "An Explanation for Public Provision of Schooling," *Journal of Law and Economics* 33, no. 1 (1990): 199–232. See also Ernest Barker, *The Development of Public Services in Western Europe* (London: Oxford University Press, 1944).

10. See Milton Friedman, *Capitalism and Freedom* (Chicago, Illinois: University of Chicago Press, 1962), 85–107. As James Poterba remarks, however, the alleged positive externalities that Friedman uses to justify public education itself, have never been demonstrated. See Poterba, "Government Intervention in the Markets for Education and Health Care: How and Why?" in *Individual and Social Responsibility: Child Care, Education, Medical Care, and Long-Term Care in America*, ed. Victor R. Fuchs (Chicago: University of Chicago Press, 1966).

11. Herbert J. Walberg, *School Choice: The Findings* (Washington, DC: The Cato Institute, 2007), 53, citing a study by Andrew Coulson. Walberg also reports that the public schools in Chile are also given extra funding for poorer students, giving private schools a competitive disadvantage in attracting such students.

12. Patrick J. McEwan, "The Effectiveness of Public, Catholic, and non- Religious Private Schools in Chile's Voucher System," *Education Economics* 9 (2001): 103–128.

13. Gregory Elacqua, Dante Contreras, and Felipe Salazar, "Scaling Up in Chile," *Education Next* 8, no. 3 (Summer 2008): 62–68, particularly 62.

14. In their Figure 2 (66), Elacqia. Contreras and Salazar break the percentages down by types of school.

15. Walberg, 51, Note 41.

16. John McClaughry, "Who Says Vouchers Don't Work?" *Reason* (January 1984): 24–32, 176.

17. Joshua Angrist, Eric Bettinger, Erik Bloom, Elizabeth King, and Michael Kremer, "Vouchers for Private Schooling in Colombia: Evidence from a Randomized Natural Experiment," *The American Economic Review* 92, no. 5 (December 2002): 1535–58.

18. Having arrived at this economic and anthropological interpretation of the central significance of the development of property rights to the advance of civilization on my own, I was irritated to discover that I was simply reinventing a wheel already invented by Herold Demsetz. See his "The Late Arrival of Capitalism," in Herold Demsetz, *From Economic Man to Economic System* (Cambridge, MA: Cambridge University Press, 2008), 65–82.

19. This same transformation in the American economy over the period 1840 through 1989 is illustrated starkly in the Council of Economic Advisers, *Economic Report of the President* (Washington, DC: U.S. Government Printing Office, February 1991), 114.

20. This process of largely eliminating feudal mercantile institutions and establishing a competitive market economy involved significant struggle and time, even in America, which

never had feudal land tenure or a mercantile system established there by the British the way the Spanish and Portuguese did in their Latin American colonies. See James Rolph Edwards, "Mercantilism, Corporations, and Liberty: The fallacies of 'Lochnerian' Antitrust," *Libertarian Papers* 1, no. 30 (2009): 1–14, particularly 5–14.

21. K. William Easter, et al., "Water Markets: Transactions Costs and Institutional Options," in *Markets for Water: Potential and Performance*, eds. K. William Easter, Ariel Dinar, and Mark W. Rosengrant (Boston, MA: Kluwer Academic Publishers,1998), 1–18, and Terry L. Anderson, "Water, Water Everywhere, But Not a Drop to Sell," in *The State of Humanity*, ed. Julian L. Simon, (Malden MA: Blackwell Publishers, 1997), 424–433.

22. Anderson, 431.

23. Easter, Dinar, and Rosengrant, 7–11.

24. Robert R. Hearne, "Institutional and Organizational Arrangements for Water Markets in Chile," in *Markets for Water: Potential and Performance*, eds. K. William Easter, Ariel Dinar, and Mark W. Rosengrant (Boston, MA: Kluwer Academic Publishers, 1998), 141– 157, particularly 142–144.

25. Robert R. Hearn and K. William Easter, "Economic and Financial Returns from Chile's Water Markets," in *Markets for Water: Potential and Performance*, eds. K. William Easter, Ariel Dinar, and Mark W. Rosengrant, (Boston, MA: Kluwer Academic Publishers, 1998), 161– 171.

26. Pinsent   Masons   Water   Yearbook,   2010–2011,   available   at   http:// www.globalwaterintel.com/pinsent-masons-yearbook/2010-2011/part2/25/.

Chapter Six

End of the Liberation Government

One more act of the military government, central to its ambitious effort to transform Chilean thinking and establish Chile as a free society, deserves special discussion. Beginning in 1976, the Chicago Boys, in and outside the government, undertook a sustained project of educating the Chilean public on the basic principles of economics and of a free society.[1] Though there certainly were those remaining on the Chilean left who undertook to dispute their assertions and arguments, their effort was, of course, made easier by the governmental suppression of the most radical elements on the left. The quality of the arguments of the Chicago Boys was very high, and the performance of the economy in the years following the 1975 recession added strength to their views. In 1980, confident that both the intellectual and policy groundwork had successfully been laid, the Pinochet government attempted a fundamental institutional reform by proposing a new constitution for Chile.

The proposed constitution was patterned to some degree after the U.S. constitution, with separation of powers between executive, legislative, and judicial branches.[2] It proposed a bicameral congress with a Senate as the upper house and a Chamber of Deputies as the lower. The executive branch was to be headed by a president, directly elected by an absolute majority. This provision was clearly designed to prevent another plurality president such as Allende. Each president would hold office for a single eight-year term. To strengthen the separation of legislative and executive powers, the allocation of expenditures was to be granted exclusively to the executive branch. Also, the constitution would make Chilean Central Bank independent of the government and *forbid it entirely* from monetizing government debt, thereby severely reducing government incentives for income redistribution and inflationary monetary policy.[3]

Perhaps the most crucial component of the proposed constitution, however, was to establish a timetable for the end of the military Junta itself and return to a multiparty republican government in 1990, through democratic elections to be held in 1989. A national plebiscite, an inherently democratic process, was to be held to consider adoption or rejection of the constitution. The Junta organized the plebiscite, campaigned for adoption of the proposed constitution, and won with just a hair over two-thirds of Chilean voters in support.[4] It should be stressed that all of this began in 1980, in only the seventh year of military rule, though some pacification of the communist left was still continuing. This was, however, also during a long economic expansion that was obviously a result of the government program of (classical) liberal, free-market reforms. And it occurred before the severe recession of 1982–1983 that cast doubt once again, for a time, on the efficacy of those reforms.

Much has been made of the fact that Pinochet seems to have had reservations about the return to democracy, or at least about leaving power himself. As with so much else that Pinochet did at this time and later in his life, almost certainly this was from a justifiable fear of retaliation by his enemies if and when that occurred, and an acutely felt need to protect himself and his family. In any case, under transitional provisions of the 1980 constitution itself, another plebiscite was scheduled for 1988, the issue of which was whether or not he would continue as president for an eight-year term, through 1997, under the newly established republic.

Such second thoughts by Pinochet may also have partly been reinforced by the discovery in 1986, by Chilean security forces, of over 80 tons of military weapons at the small fishing harbor of Carrizal Bajo. The weapons had been smuggled into Chile by the armed branch of the outlawed Chilean communist party known as the Manuel Rodriguez Patriotic Front (FPMR) with the aid of Cuba, East Germany, and the USSR.[5] This danger was reinforced in September of that year when weapons from the same source were used in an assassination attempt by the FPMR against Pinochet himself, in which five of his military bodyguards were killed and the General barely escaped.[6]

Under this state of affairs, it is not surprising that Pinochet attempted to retain office in 1988. What is striking, though, is that *he did so through a democratic process*. Even more striking, in 1987, the year after the assassination attempt and the year before the national plebiscite, he legalized the formation and operation of political parties again, and when the vote of the plebiscite itself came in with almost 60 percent against him retaining the presidency, he left power along with the rest of the military government as scheduled in his own constitution. Even here he took measures to protect himself. Pinochet remained Commander-in-Chief of the army until 1998 and was then, under provisions of the 1980 constitution, made a senator for life, a position under which he was immune from prosecution for his actions as head of the military liberation government.

REBIRTH OF THE CHILEAN REPUBLIC

Political parties quickly reemerged when the military government made it legal for them to do so in 1987. A coalition of center-left parties, including the Christian Democrats, the Socialist Party, and the Radical Party, then formed to promote a vote of "no" in the 1988 plebiscite on Pinochet's retention of the presidency of Chile. People were eager for an end to military rule, perhaps precisely because, like the government itself, most had come to recognize the benefits of the free market reforms, and thought that democracy could work without reverting to the destructive rent-seeking and redistributive politics of the past. So, of course, the "no" vote won. The coalition then negotiated with the military government for a set of amendments to the 1980 constitution designed to enhance constitutional rights, limit the power of government by restricting state of emergency declarations, and alter the amendment procedure itself. Many of the proposals were accepted.

In 1990, the center-left coalition (by then formally known as the Coalition of Parties for Democracy, or *Concertacion* for short), gaining further support from several smaller parties, put forward Patricio Aylwin for President, along with a list of legislative candidates. Aylwin was opposed by Hernan Buchi, a Chicago-Boy candidate of a smaller center-right coalition of parties, who had been Pinochet's Finance Minister since 1985. Buchi ended up getting only 30 percent of the vote, with 55 percent going to Aylwin, and the remainder to a third candidate. *Concertacion* also won a majority of votes for parliament, though due to the representation system embodied in the 1980 constitution, they did not achieve an absolute majority of seats, and had to negotiate legislation with the center-right coalition.

The extent of the ideological change that had by this time already been wrought in Chile, needs to be stressed. The ideological outcome of the prior events, including: physical removal of the most radical of the left from Chilean society; the demonstrated economic success of the free market reforms; Pinochet's clear willingness to establish a new constitution and leave office; and the systematic efforts of the Chicago Boys to explain the institutions of a free society, was to move opinion on both the right and the left toward broad acceptance of the liberal institutions and policies of a free society. Both the center-left and center-right groups came to share that view. This convergence is attested to (though bitterly lamented) by the remaining intellectual opponents of the market reforms.[7] It is also attested to by the steady advance of such reforms under all the democratically elected governments that have thus far followed. The forward march of free market policies has been remarkable.

Consider the Aylwin government. Rather than reverting to the policies of nationalization, income redistribution, import substitution, and politicization of society employed by Chilean governments prior to the 1973 military takeover, the Aylwin government seemed to exhibit an excitement for free-market experiments to test the limits and further diminish the role of the state. In 1991, for example, the government passed a law allowing *private* sector participation in the development of what is normally thought of as *public* infrastructure, including the building and operation of roads, airports, and seaports.[8]

Just as remarkable as its extensions of the private sector was fiscal discipline of the Aylwin government. Social spending did rise by some 3.4 percent in its 1990–1991 budget, yet the administration controlled overall expenditures tightly and ran a surplus in the budget equal to 2.5 percent of GDP, as shown and referenced in Figure 3.4. This discipline, which has held through every administration since, is not just a matter of self-control by officials, of course. The fact that, under the 1980 constitution, they cannot now run debts and pressure the Central Bank to purchase the government securities has been a major factor in maintaining this discipline. Also, the commitments made under the social security law were restraining. Yet clearly, intentions by both the center-left and the center-right to keep welfare state activity to a minimum and rely more on the *productive* generation of wealth have been important.

The Aylwin government demonstrated that intention even in its labor policy, an amazing fact given the strength of unions in the *Concertacion* constituency. Though it did relax some of the limits placed on union activity by the military government, in April of 1991 the Aylwin administration, in negotiations with major business and labor groups, got them to accept that future increases in the minimum wage would be tied to productivity increases. As Valesco points out, this was a major step toward breaking indexation to prior inflation and instituting meaningful flexibility in wage rates.[9] This was probably a significant factor in the reduction of inflation rates to single-digit levels that occurred during the Aylwin years, as shown in Figure 3.2.

In 1994, Aylwin stepped aside and was succeeded as President by Eduardo Frei Ruiz-Tagle, son of the earlier Chilean President. Like his father, Frei was a member of the PDC, and he ran as the *Concertacion* candidate, winning and holding the Presidency until the year 2000. With a sharp departure showing just how far attitudes had moved from the policies of his father, however, the new Frei government passed a law his first year in office permitting free entry by private firms into the long-distance telecommunications industry that had previously been maintained as a government franchised monopoly. That legal change resulted in a rush of private entry into the business, adding to competitive supply and causing a large reduction in long-distance telephone rates.[10]

The Frei government also oversaw other notable market liberalizing reforms. One was a reduction in banking regulation in 1997 extending the types of loans banks could make. Also, continuing the movement toward free trade, the government passed a law unilaterally and automatically reducing the import tariff rate by one percentage point per year, to end in 2003 when it reached 6 percent.[11] Unfortunately, Frei's tenure was marred by a recession in 1999 that hurt his popularity. It was very mild compared to those of 1975 and 1982–1983, and the economy quickly resumed growth.

Changes in Central Bank policy over the 1990s should also be mentioned, since they had an important effect on national economic performance. Having been made independent of the government and denied the power to monetize debt by the 1980 constitution, the military government had further reformed its operations in 1989 by restricting the Bank's statutory objectives and authority to stabilizing prices, the domestic payment system, and Chile's external payments.

In 1991, the Bank adopted inflation rate targeting as its primary operating procedure, with a progressively widening foreign exchange rate band. Within that band, the foreign exchange rate was determined by world market supply and demand conditions, and only when the rate went outside the band did the Bank intervene. In 1999, the band was essentially abolished altogether, with the Bank promising to intervene only in an emergency.[12] *Thus floating exchange rates were progressively, incrementally established over the 1990s.* This has allowed the Bank greater control over the domestic money supply, and along with the labor maret reform discussed above, had a great deal to do with allowing the Bank to reduce Chilean inflation rates to low single digits.

Cumulatively, the economic effects of this fiscal and monetary discipline and ongoing pro-market reforms through the first three center-left democratic administrations were astounding. By the mid-1990s, the unemployment rate was at very low historic levels, as shown and referenced earlier in Figure 3.4. For the ten years from 1991 through 2000 Central Bank data shows that real Chilean GDP grew at an average compound annual rate of over 6.4 percent.[13] Even with the 1999 recession, this raised real production and income by over 64 percent. Population grew, but per capita real income still increased so rapidly that Chile's poverty rate fell from 33 percent of the population in the early '90s to only 17 percent by the year 2000, a decline of nearly 49 percent. Over this period, the average poverty rate among Latin nations generally only fell from 41 to 36 percent, a mere 12.2 percent reduction.[14]

The year 2000 Presidential election was won by Ricardo Lagos, another center-left candidate, this time in a tight race with Joaquin Lavin Infante, the center-right candidate. Many people called Lagos the first avowedly leftist president since Allende. During his term a national unemployment insurance system was instituted, compulsory education was extended to 12 years, and Chile's first divorce law was passed. However, even Lagos openly supported and extended the market reform agenda that has been adhered to since the Pinochet years. During 2002, Chile negotiated a free trade agreement with the European Union. In 2003 Chile signed one with the U.S., and in 2004 signed another with South Korea. Despite suffering a scandal in early 2002 in which it was discovered that ministers in his government were being given payments in addition to their regular salaries, Lagos finished his term with high public approval ratings. [15]

Michelle Bachelet, the committed socialist who succeeded Lagos in 2006 and was the first Chilean President since the rebirth of the Republic to have a majority in both chambers of Congress, rolled a few of the market reforms back marginally and instituted a few modest income redistributions. Those included provision of daycare for poor children, housing subsidies for low-income Chileans, a controversial decree providing for distribution of the "morning-after" pill to women older than 14 *without* parental consent, and a few others. [16] However, in keeping with the now ingrained Chilean free trade policy, her government concluded multilateral trade deals with New Zealand, Singapore and several other nations in 2006 and free trade agreements with Japan and India in 2007. Indeed, in early 2010, Chile was allowed to become the 31st member of the Organization for Economic Cooperation and Development (OECD), the exclusive club of the world's high-income nations. [17]

In comparison to the 1985–2000 period, economic growth was lower and unemployment rates rather high under both Lagos and Bachelet (Figures 3.3 and 3.4) and the Chilean public was ready for a change. Bachelet was succeeded in 2010 by Sebastian Pinera. Pinera, the economist, who as mentioned earlier is the younger brother of Jose Pinera and is a wealthy entrepreneur. Pinera became the first elected Presidential candidate from the center-right coalition. The Chicago Boys are, as of this writing, in control again, and this time, with the expressed consent of the franchised electorate.

Pinera has already achieved both worldwide recognition and almost heroic status within Chile for his role in the rescue of the 33 Chilean miners from Copiapo who were trapped far underground on August 5, 2010. [18] The effort led by Pinera and his Mining Minister, Laurence Golborne, resulted in the miners being brought safely above ground by October 13th, more than two months earlier than the initial estimates. As Pinera's government develops its policies, innovative extensions of the free society that has been building in Chile since the original Chicago Boys came to power may well occur. In any case, both serious socialism and the import substitution policy of the Chilean left are dead, and good riddance.

Also dead is the pervasive misallocation of resources away from productive uses and into rent-seeking political activities that so marked and marred

Chilean society before the military coup. It was killed by the shift of so many functions and resources away from the government to the private sector. Now, as long as the government performs its legitimate functions of preventing predatory activities (theft, murder, fraud, etc.) and enforcing voluntary contracts, incomes largely have to be earned through productive actions and voluntary exchanges.

PROSECUTION AND/OR PERSECUTION

Given the sustained commitment of both the center-left and center-right co-alitions in Chile to (classical) liberal market institutions since the end of the military government, an outsider might ask what issues divide the two. Aside from mild social-democratic rhetoric and a progressive legislative agenda on the left and a somewhat greater commitment to strictly limited government on the right, the primary difference has been the support and affection for Pinochet on the right and the bitter hatred of him by members of the left. Through center-left dominated governments over nearly twenty years, re-peated, ongoing efforts were made to build a case and find a way to prosecute Pinochet for the violent suppressive actions his government took against Chilean communists and their allies.

Those efforts to prosecute Pinochet were just as persistently opposed by members of the center-right opposition who idolize him. They believed—and still believe—that he saved the nation from a totalitarian disaster that would have begun with far worse and more widespread suppression, murder, and torture than Pinochet inflicted, *conducted precisely by many of those he suppressed*, and that, as such, his actions were both necessary and largely justified. His supporters also believe, and quite correctly, that the capitalist, free-market policies of Pinochet and the Chicago economists generated the prosperity and freedom that Chileans quickly came to enjoy. Such prosperity and freedom was *never* experienced by *any* of the *communist* nations of the 20th century.[19]

Pinochet's enemies had two initial tasks before they could prosecute him. First was to document cases of murder, torture, assassination, and other human rights abuses by the military government, and propagate them widely to build public support. Second, they had to find ways around the legal immunity that Pinochet had granted himself, that *Concertacion* itself had accepted in negotiations for the transition to democracy. This first task was not hard because commissions set up by the U.N. and other international agencies had already documented many human rights abuses by the Pinochet government in reports, such as the Inter-American Commission on Human Rights report released in 1986.

Many Chileans—more than a few of whom would have felt very little moral outrage had it been their side doing the murders, assassinations and torturing against "capitalist oppressors" and "enemies of the people"—were eager to tell horror stories about the actions of the military government.[20] Accordingly, in 1991 the Aylwin government created the misnamed Rhettig Commission on Peace and Reconciliation to gather evidence. The commission reported in 1993, setting off widespread public debate and dissension. Other commissions were subsequently formed and gave their reports, such as the Valech Report of 1994, giving the left more of the evidence needed to make its case in the court of public opinion, if not in the courts of law.

Since Pinochet's immunity extended only to the Chilean legal system, one way to prosecute him would be to use an outside jurisdiction. In 1998, Pinochet, his health beginning to fail, went to Britain for medical treatment. In an act of perfidy with enormous implications for international relations, the British authorities arrested him on October 17th on a Spanish provisional warrant for the alleged murder of Spanish citizens while he was president. A few days later he was served with another provisional arrest warrant issued by a Spanish judge. Fighting his arrest and incarceration in the British courts for nearly two years, Pinochet was finally released in March of 2000 by the British Home Secretary, Jack Straw, without ever having come to trial for the alleged murders.[21]

Pinochet arrived back home to the acclaim of his friends and protests of his enemies. Still in ill health and obviously declining, his opponents seem to have grown increasingly desperate to convict him of something. They contrived a subtle strategy. In the same month he arrived home, March of 2000, the center-left dominated Congress, by a large majority, voted to create a condition of ex-President granting immunity from prosecution to those having that status. To obtain this status, however, Pinochet had to give up his seat of senator-for-life. Judge Juan Guzman Tapia then initiated a procedure against him, requesting suspension of his promised immunity.

In August of that year, the Supreme Court of Chile ruled in favor of Guzman's request, removing Pinochet's congressional immunity by a vote of 14-6.[22] In December Pinochet was indicted for "kidnapping" many communist and radical-left leaders in the Caravan of Death case.[23] The charge of kidnapping was applied because murder could not be proved since the bodies were missing. In 2002, the Supreme Court dismissed the indictment because of Pinochet's failing health, but then reversed itself in 2004, holding that he was fit to stand trial after all. In 2005, Pinochet was indicted on tax evasion charges and placed under house arrest.

The next year, Pinochet was indicted for kidnapping and tortures conducted at the Via Grimaldi Detention Center and for the 1995 assassination of biochemist Eugenio Berrios, who had long been claimed to have been complicit with Pinochet in many tortures and murders.[24] Apparently, it was believed that Pinochet had Berrios murdered to silence him. Pinochet's enemies had begun efforts to prosecute him on other matters as well. Accusations of drug trafficking were made against both Pinochet himself and members of his family, though his son, Marco Antonio, sued Manuel Contreras, one of the main accusers, for libel.

Influential men of the left in America added their effort to this struggle. In 2004 a subcommittee of the U.S. Senate Finance Committee led by Carl Levin (D-MI), charged with investigating compliance of financial institutions under the USA PATRIOT Act, claimed that it found a network of some 125 bank accounts at the Riggs Bank tied to Pinochet through aliases and associates.[25] Though such hearsay evidence and assertions of guilt-by-association were less than convincing, they were certainly inflammatory, and hence led to more charges and investigations of tax evasion, fraud, and money laundering against Pinochet and his family living in Chile. Investigations and indictments against Pinochet for murders and tortures occurring under the military government also continued. Apparently the legal immunity of ex-President status meant much less than Pinochet had been lead to believe.

Though efforts to prosecute his family continue to this day, the efforts against Pinochet himself came to naught. On December 3, 2006, he suffered a heart attack and died, without ever having been proven guilty of anything in any court of law. Almost certainly, of course, he was guilty of many crimes against humanity. Normal legal procedures are always suspended in conditions of emergency and overt conflict, even in the most civilized of nations. Still, the military government should have given fair trials to those it suspected of sedition and/or treason before executing or imprisoning those found guilty, even if such trials were held in military courts. They should also have eschewed the use of torture in gaining evidence, however desperate they believed the situation to be at the time.

In fairness it must be remembered that the level of casualties in the revolutionary insurgence of September 1974 and the subsequent struggle to pacify the armed militias, leadership, and other luminaries of the UP, was actually very *small*, in the historical context of Latin American Revolutions. Rather than acting without restraint against the forces (armed, political, and intellectual) of the radical left, the liberation government clearly exercised a great deal of self-restraint. The continued existence, over its whole tenure, and to this day, of a very large number of leftist academics, artists, and intellectuals in Chile able to complain publicly of the abuses of the liberation government itself testifies of that restraint.

It is difficult to imagine the horror of life under the Pinochet government for those on the left who were tortured, imprisoned, or lived in fear of the infliction of such things. However, a few of the leftist commentators who obsess over this horror have ever bothered to recognize the horror of life under *Allende* for those who were tortured by *his* security thugs, or for the many who lived in fear day after day, wondering if their lands or business livelihood would soon be confiscated. Likewise, such analysts ignore the anguish millions of Chileans felt over whether there would be food or other necessities of life on the shelves next week, or whether they would be killed when the communists completed their takeover, or—if they were lucky— merely have to live a servile life of poverty under totalitarian tyranny.[26] It really is sad when the intended oppressors of a nation become so powerful that their intended victims become convinced that it is necessary to turn oppression on them.

With the coup, the vast majority of Chileans found themselves *liberated* as communist tyranny was averted, the coercive hand of the state was steadily *diminished* in society, private property was restored and extended, and personal rights of self-determination, free association, and voluntary contract were established and protected in the law. In defense against charges that he had been a dictator, Pinochet once asked, in essence, what kind of dictator it is that leaves power voluntarily? He might just as well have asked what kind of dictator it was that saves a nation from communist totalitarianism, has its people taught the principles of a free-society, establishes the fundamental constitutional and institutional structure of such a society, enacts policies that soon make its people the most prosperous in the region, and voluntarily restores a vastly improved republic. What kind indeed?

NOTES

1. Valdez, 28.
2. Unlike the U.S. Constitution, however, which was written by representatives sent by preexisting states, the Pinochet constitution did not establish a federal system of government. In Chile, the geographic sub-units are under control of the central government.
3. Corbo and Hernandez, 128–129.
4. Rex A. Hudson, ed., *Chile: A Country Study* (Washington, DC: U.S. Government Printing Office for the Library of Congress, 1995), and Loveman, 288.
5. "Manuel Rodriguez Patriotic Front," *Wikipedia* (23 August 2010).
6. "1986: Pinochet Survives Rebel Ambush," *BBC* (8 September 2006).
7. See, for example, Petras and Vieux, *The Chilean Economic Miracle: an Empirical Critique*, 65–66, where they complain that even many of the analysts from whom they had derived their data criticizing the policies and accomplishments of the military government had come to accept the neoliberal ideology and then jumped ship, joining the Aylwin government and supporting its continuance of (classical) liberal policies.
8. Corbo and Hernandez, 131.
9. Valesco, 410.
10. Corbo and Hernandez, 131.
11. Corbo and Hernendez, 136.
12. Corbo and Hernendez, 131.
13. Esteban Jadresic and Roberto Zahler, "Chile's Rapid Growth in the 1990s: Good Luck, Good Policies, or Political Change?" *International Monetary Fund Working Paper* (October 2000), looking at a slightly different interval, find that the growth of real GDP in Chile from 1990 to 1998 was above 7 percent per year, and affirm that this was higher than that achieved

by *any* other Latin nation. Econometrically testing the hypothesis that this outstanding performance was simply a matter of luck, they reject that claim, finding instead that it was due to good economic policies and improved political institutions rooted in the reforms of the 1970s and 1980s.

14. Jadresic and Zahler, 133.

15. "Ricardo Lagos," *Wikipedia* (17 January 2011).

16. She was able to obtain this congressional majority due to a constitutional reform under Lagos that eliminated the provision in the 1980 constitution for appointed Senators which had enhanced the legislative strength of the right.

17. "Michelle Bachelet," Wikipedia (2 August 2010).

18. "Chile's textbook mine rescue brings global respect," Associated Press (13 October, 2010).

19. One might think this assertion refuted by the rapid economic growth currently being experienced by mainland China and Vietnam. But Red China is no longer *Red* in terms of its economic policies, nor is Vietnam. Both have established capitalist market economies. On China, see Wing Thye Woo, "The Experimentalist-Convergence Debate on Interpreting China's Economic Growth: A Cross-Country Perspective," in, *Living Standards and the Wealth of Nations,* eds. Leszek Balcerowicz and Stanley Fischer (Cambridge, MA: MIT Press, 2006), 73–113. On Vietnam, see William Ratliff, *Vietnam Rising* (Oakland CA.: The Independent Institute, 2008).

20. Andrew and Mitrokhin, 87–88, give a damning comparison. Just at the time that Operation Toucan was successfully exaggerating the atrocities committed by the Pinochet regime, Pol Pot and his communist Khmer Rouge were conducting a reign of terror in which they murdered at least 1.5 *million* Cambodians out of an initial population of only 7.5 million. Yet, The *New York Times,* in 1976, published sixty-six articles on human rights abuses under Pinochet, but only *four* on the slaughter and oppression conducted by the communist government in Cambodia.

21. British Broadcasting Company, "Pinochet Set Free" (2 March 2000).

22. Loveman, 358.

23. BBC, "Pinochet Charged with Kidnapping" (1 December 2000).

24. BBC, "Court Lifts Pinochet Immunity" (8 September 2006).

25. United States Senate Permanent Subcommittee on Investigations of the Committee on Governmental Affairs: "Levin-Coleman Staff Report Discloses Web of Secret Accounts Used by Pinochet", press release.

26. For documentation of the atrocities committed by virtually all of the communist governments of the 20th century see Stephane Courtios, Nicolas Werth, Jean-Louis Panne, Andrzej Paczkowski, Karel Bartosek, and Jean Louis Margolin, *The Black Book of Communism* (Cambridge, MA: Harvard University Press, 1999). For a very brief summary see Lee Edwards, "Still Bowing to the God that Failed," *The Intercollegiate Review* (Fall/Winter 2004): 3–12.

About the Author

James Rolph Edwards obtained his Bachelor of Science degree in Political Science from Brigham Young University in 1968. While at B.Y.U., he organized and ran the university Kodokan Judo club, teaching lessons and introducing many students to that competitive art, though he was only a Ni-Kyu brown belt at the time. After a stint in the army, where he spent nine months on the 8th Armored Division pistol team in Germany, he returned home, took up Judo competition again, and earned his Sho-Dan. In 1971, Edwards married Marilyn Nielson, of Ephraim, Utah, and a few years later he began taking economics courses at the University of Utah. Edwards was awarded his Ph.D. in economics in 1983, with specialized fields in Industrial Organization and International Monetary Theory. That same year, he became the Ludwig von Mises Assistant Professor of Economics at Hillsdale College in Michigan. From1988 to the present, Dr. Edwards has taught economics and political science continuously at Montana State University-Northern, in Havre, where he achieved the rank of Full Professor. Over the years he has written several books and many journal articles on economic topics, along with one novel.